THE ART OF MAKING DANCES

The Art of Making Dances

by DORIS HUMPHREY

EDITED BY BARBARA POLLACK

A Dance Horizons Book
Princeton Book Company / Princeton, NJ

A Dance Horizons Book
Princeton Book Company, Publishers
POB 831
Hightstown, NJ 08520-0831

Grateful acknowledgement is made to John Malcom Brinnin for permission to reprint a brief selection from his poem, "Death of This Death" from *The Garden is Political;* and to Doubleday & Company, Inc. for permission to reprint four lines from "The Lost Son" in *The Lost Son and Other Poems,* by Theodore Roethke, copyright 1947 by The University of the South.

Line drawings by Stuyvesant Van Veen
Cover design by Janet Hautau

Manufactured in the United States of America

LC#   59-6573
ISBN: 0-87127-158-3

Grateful acknowledgment for help in preparation of this book is made to Mr. and Mrs. José Limón, Martha Hill, Ruth Currier, Merrill Pollack, Henry Moscow, Lydia Joel and Mr. and Mrs. James Payton.

Foreword

I think the germ of this book must have existed a very long time ago indeed, probably back to the time when I was a very small child and heard my mother playing MacDowell's "Witches' Dance" and Sinding's "Rustle of Spring" as I was going to sleep. Also, about this time, I heard Bach's "Air for the G String," which so struck me to the heart that it was almost the first dance I composed as an independent choreographer. Then there was that exquisite Christmas song that used to melt me, "Lo How a Rose E'er Blooming."

So music was my first love and I was led to dance through that, although I was a miserable failure at playing any of it myself at the keyboard. I am reminded of Mozart, who said that he really cared more for dancing than for music, and surely his music dances as living proof of his devotion. But I came to love dancing very much, almost as much as music, and went through a number of stages of development, notably in choreography, to the point where I have at last put down on paper my ideas about the art of making dances. Still I think I should have preferred to be a composer of music.

In the effort to commit my theory to paper, I must first thank the John Simon Guggenheim Memorial Foundation, who gave me a Fellowship for this project well over ten years ago, and who have waited patiently for the outcome without any signs of frowns or annoyance. Then there are the hundreds of students and professional dancers who have served as guinea pigs for experimental ideas in choreography, and who, I hope, were rewarded then, and will also now be able to see some of the results of their labors in this book. But my deepest gratitude goes to my husband, Charles Francis Woodford, who stood by me in famine and in feast, and who always believed that I could make more dances, think more creative thoughts and write this book.

DORIS HUMPHREY

October 11, 1958
New York City

Contents

One

AN INTRODUCTION
TO CHOREOGRAPHY

. . . Shut up the words, and seal the book, even to the time of the end: many shall run to and fro, and knowledge shall be increased.

Daniel 12:4

The Sleeping Beauty

1 The dance has been, until recently, entirely ingenue, a sweet obedient child brought up in the theater and the court, and told to be young, pretty and amusing. Steps and whole dances were borrowed for this infant from the lower classes (who were really inventive), and had their vulgarities removed so that kings and courtiers might find them acceptable for both performing and viewing. Naturally the communal form of the folk dance was rejected, and all dances took on the attributes of regal society. Plot, when needed, was patterned after drama, but only the lighter and more whimsical forms were used. The drama was interrupted by display pieces of technique, thought to be much more important than the story. All had to be airy, charming, with sadness the mere shadow of a butterfly's wing. *Le roi s'amuse.* A very brief glance at some operas and dramas which were contemporaneous with typical ballets will illustrate the light attitude taken toward the dance. Serious subject matter, always acceptable in drama and opera, was unthinkable in respect to the ballet — Donizetti's "Lucia di Lammermoor" was produced in 1835; Adolphe Adam's ephemeral "Giselle" in 1851. When Tschaikovsky wrote his opera "Eugen Onegin" in 1879 it was stern stuff, but in 1877 he composed the famous "Swan Lake" and thirteen years later the fairy tale, "The Sleeping Beauty." At about the same time, Ibsen wrote *The Pillars of Society* and *Ghosts.*

This is not to say that the ballet form was bad, but only that it was limited and suffered from arrested development—a permanent sixteen, like the Sleeping Beauty herself. So well established was the formula over so many hundreds of years that, as the twentieth century dawned with its flood of new ideas, there was considerable resistance to any change from the light love story and the fairy tale, and there still is.

Beginning in 1900, the fresh influences at work were many. Isadora Duncan removed story from the dance altogether and insisted that the dance could be an emanation of the soul and the emotions. Ruth St. Denis and Ted Shawn proclaimed religious experience and ritual as valid among a host of other new subject matter, and psychological discoveries introduced profoundly new ways of dealing with character and drama. Social changes revolutionized the ancient king, queen and courtier forms, so that the corps de ballet often became a group composed entirely of solo dancers, with no king and queen in sight. Suddenly the dance, the Sleeping Beauty, so long reclining in her dainty bed, had risen up with a devouring desire. No Prince Charming was the answer. She awoke staring into the muzzles of the guns of World War I, and she was enamored of such unlikely things as machinery (mechanistic ballets), social problems, ancient ritual and nature (flowers, bees, water, wolves). Another surprising development was her taste for comedy and satire. Not just bits of caricature like that of the elderly lecher in the romantic tale, but full-fledged ballets, humorous and sophisticated. She changed her attitude toward music—the "Dance of the Hours" was certainly not suited to all her moods—and she demanded serious consideration from serious composers. Occasionally she even banished all music or went in for sound effects and odd instruments. Her contacts with the other arts produced changes, too, notably with architecture, as reflected especially in stage design; and literature, which gave her new ideas about form and content. In short, those concerned with the welfare of the awakening beauty thought she should abandon her ingenuous ways and grow up.

In the first half of the twentieth century, the dance expanded and experimented in so many directions that a mere listing of them would demand too much time. The changes in the art have been more startling, more sudden and more numerous than those in any other field. They include radical differences in technique, style, form and content, and most welcome and surprising of all, several theories of choreography.

Man has composed dances throughout the ages, from the earliest prehistoric era to the present time, but it was only in the nineteen thirties that theories of dance composition were developed and taught. Previously dance was all composed instinctively, or with the natural talent of the composer. Dance has done extraordinarily well for itself without theory, by virtue of the efforts of gifted individuals who, up to recent times, had no framework to work within, such as music had with its counterpoint and harmony, or painting with its laws of perspective and proportion. The lack of a body of theory for so many hundreds of years seems to present three points for speculation. First, since dance has flourished very well without rules or guides for composition, why do we need any now? And second, since the other arts have always abounded in intellectual analysis and ideas about form, why was the dance devoid of these until fairly recently? And lastly, why was there a sudden development of theory in the thirties?

On the first point, it hardly seems necessary to defend so obvious an aid to art as a theory of craftsmanship. One can only imagine what the state of drama would be without it (as long ago as Aeschylus, there were rules for drama), or music (think of it without theory after the troubadour stage) or any of the other arts. I believe we can dismiss as highly naïve any contention that we cannot benefit from compositional techniques or that these cannot be taught in the dance. This would be tantamount to saying that intellectual effort and analysis, though valuable in all other kinds of human activity, are without function or necessity in this one area of one art.

On the second point, that there were no theoreticians of form up to 1930, I have one basic explanation, the physicality of the art. Movement is its essence, its keynote and its language. The person drawn to dance as a profession is notoriously unintellectual. He thinks with his muscles; delights in expression with body, not words; finds analysis painful and boring; and is a creature of physical ebullience. Since there were always a few gifted individuals who would undertake to put dances together and had a knack for dramatic sequence, everyone else was content to let well enough alone and depend on a few choreographers and their flashes of inspiration. There was one other element which had a bearing on the situation. Very early in the Renaissance there began to be a body of tradition in the dance, especially as to technique; rules of movement were handed down from one century to another with slight divergences, and there emerged an Italian School and a French School. Reverence for the tenets of these traditions was fierce and partisan, and was highly conducive to an acquiescent state of mind, where independent thinking was frowned on. One of the greatest hindrances to deviation from the status quo was the cold fact that the tradition in schools and ballet companies was crown-supported and any rebel was out of a job. A theory of composition was not in the tradition, and therefore did not exist. All this continued for some four hundred years, until there occurred several jolting shocks in quick succession.

One of these was the revelation of new conceptions of dance brought to Europe by Ruth St. Denis and Isadora Duncan at the turn of the century. This effectively loosened the rigid formulas, especially in Russia, and inspired Michel Fokine in his famous revolt. Fokine rebelled against the stilted and artificial ways of the Russian Imperial Ballet and School. He declared that dancers should look like human beings, that technique should vary according to the theme, and that music and décor should correspond in style to the period chosen. Not long after came the Russian Revolution, which displaced so many of the fine dancers and choreographers, leading them to a new evaluation of their art. However, this did not yet produce a theory of choreography. This was reserved, in my opinion, for the emotional climate that followed the first World War, and leads me to my third point.

Why did choreographic theory suddenly emerge in the nineteen thirties? It seems to me that the social upheaval of the first world cataclysm was, more than anything else, responsible for the emergence of a compositional theory. The shocks reached all the way down to the thoughtless lives of dancers, especially in America. Everything was re-evaluated in the light of the violence and the terrible disruption, and the dance was no exception. Two centers of the world reacted especially strongly. In the United States and in Germany, dancers asked themselves some serious questions. "What am I dancing about?" "Is it worthy in the light of the kind of person I am and the kind of world I live in?" "But if not, what other kind of dance shall there be, and how should it be organized?"

The dancers in the United States took fully ten years to think about these problems, to detach themselves from the patterns of life and work which enmeshed them, and set themselves to evolve a dance of their own. I was one of the dancers who was fortunate enough to be in at the beginning of these stirring times. I began a fascinating voyage of discovery which resulted not only in a theory of movement that satisfied me, but which made me realize very early that a practical theory of composition was a necessity. This was not only because of my consuming desire to know and understand composition, but because of the many students whom I was guiding and initiating gently into the joys of individuality and independent thinking.   .

Being well aware that not all, or even a majority, of my students would want to think enough to understand or use a theory of choreography (the physicality of dancers still exists), I still could not in good conscience turn them loose without some knowledge of composition. This was particularly true because I never believed in teaching with a set vocabulary of movements, hardened into technical sequences. I always thought students should learn principles of movement and be encouraged to expand or embroider on these in their own way. So, along with a theory of movement, there was a theory of composition. It was apparent soon that choreographic ability in students was going to be very much in demand with the astonishing spread of the modern dance through the educational system. Dance teachers in colleges and studios were required to compose for their students' recitals and for drama and musical events. Many others besides myself, in various parts of the world, felt the urgency of the new attitudes and situations, and so, due to the enterprise of modern dancers, a new dimension was added to dance: a theory of choreography. The Sleeping Beauty was awake indeed.

The body of this book is a setting forth of my approach to this subject, to which I invariably add this prefix: These ideas are not intended to be a formula; they do not pretend to be a magic brew for success—I have been putting them into practice for many years and they work for me, and may work for others, provided there is that mysterious added ingredient, talent. I like to think that choreographic theory and the study of it is a craft, and only that, for I do not claim that anyone can be taught to create, but only that talent or possibly genius can be supported and informed by know-how, just as an architect, no matter how gifted, must understand the uses of steel, glass and stone.

Choreographers Are Special People

2 It is a truism that the performing arts are much richer in interpreters than in creators; the proportion is probably a hundred to one or more. Good composers, playwrights and choreographers are so obviously in the minority that, in respect to the dance, it might be well to inquire into the characteristics the would-be choreographer should have. Knowing what these are might save a good deal of grief, not only for long-suffering dancers, but for the public, the management and the choreographer himself. Certainly, without some of the traits and attitudes of the creative mind, as applied to the dance, any dancer would be ill advised to undertake such a difficult and demanding enterprise as a composing career. Also, this knowledge might give pause to those individuals who, through frustration from whatever cause, think with cheerful ignorance, "Oh, well, I'll be a choreographer," or teach children, or write ballet scenarios, or any of those so-called fringe activities which, to the uninformed, seem so much simpler than the acquiring of a performing technique.

First of all, the potential choreographer should be predominantly extrovert and a keen observer of physical and emotional behavior. Please note that the list does not begin with imagination, inspiration, improvisational skill, poetic or musical feeling, or dramatic ability, although they certainly play an important part. The dancer's medium is the body, which is an extremely practical and tangible piece of goods, much more so than words, musical notes or paint. It already has a definite shape, and is equipped with a highly complex system of levers, limbs, nerves and muscles, plus a lived-in personality with entrenched ways of its own. I should say that the first mark of the potential choreographer is a knowledge of, or at least a great curiosity about, the body—not just his own, but the heterogeneous mixture of bodies which people his environment. Then the uniqueness of each personality, beginning with his own, should ever be before him. He should be aware that he is profoundly different from his much-beloved and respected teachers and that mere imitation of them can only lead to disaster. Honesty is the prime essential here. He must ask himself, "What do I believe in, what do I want to say?" He must have a high resistance to novelty for its own sake and courage to depart from the trends of the day if necessary. To compose for himself, he must put a stethoscope to his own heart and listen to those mysterious inner voices which are the guide to originality. In composing for other dancers, he must have a high regard for their individuality, remember that they are not like himself and bring all his intelligence to bear on the problem of understanding them, physically, emotionally and psychologically These points seem almost too obvious to mention, but experience has shown that such factors are all too often missing. The many choreographic failures I have seen are due to a variety of complex causes; one of them, insensitivity to people, is the frequent villain. Many a performance brings to my mind's eye an X-ray picture of the rehearsal period. The choreographer is a solo dancer who has come to work with a bundle of material made on his own body, which he has blindly pasted on his dancers. For example: A small, compact, quick female has before her three slow-moving, statuesque girls and two six-foot men. She takes the leading part and shows them all up as bad imitations of her—with the inevitable disastrous results. Also, almost invariably, as another result of this insensitivity, the dance turns out as a solo done by six dancers at the same time, as if they were a strip of paper dolls. They are not a group at all, for this requires molding and relationships between figures—in short, choreographic shaping.

The choreographer-director who will diligently keep an open mind about his people is in for some delightful surprises, too. As I've noted earlier, the dancer is a notoriously nonverbal thinker, and inarticulate as well; therefore his everyday behavior is not a reliable clue to his potential as a performer. Give him some challenges via expressive movement and the apparently nondescript personality will often reveal hidden treasure in talent. That somnolent young man who never opens his mouth has a gift for satire! The hard-boiled technician has been concealing a romantic heart, not even suspected by herself. Incidentally, this mining for gold in personalities is one of the chief rewards of the choreographer, as thrilling as the work of other explorers and adventurers. If our hypothetical choreographer does not respond with enthusiasm to such adventure, he probably does not have the temperament for a life of composing. There is a simple test for this in the recurrent prayers of a supplicant at the altar of the dance. If these consist of pleas for a masterful technique, large aud-

iences, public acclaim at the footlights for him alone, and lots of performances and money, then the career of a dancer is clearly indicated, and any
inadvertent straying into choreography is not likely to be successful. This
is not to say that performing is inferior as an ambition, but only that it is
different from, and fully as difficult as, composing. In some rare cases, of
course, fortune pours extravagant amounts of talent into one individual
and there emerges that scintillating rarity, the performer-composer.

To consider further traits important to the choreographer: This person is not only sensitive to people but is observant in general; he is not
just interested in, but fascinated with, all manifestations of form and
shape. He notes the designs in his everyday living, wherever he may be.
In the city? He sees the architectural variations, the skyline, the tangled
grotesqueries of water tanks, television wires, ventilators, the "feel" of the
congestion, the preponderance of rectilinear lines, and the comedy of the
small defiant brownstones squashed between the mammoth chromium and
glass monsters. In the country? Nature presents a never-ending panorama
of wind and cloud, shapes of growing things, animal life, plain and mountain and water. All of this has much to teach him about form and relationships. But his greatest interest is in people. He sees people en masse, as
in a street, moving in kaleidoscopic patterns, or else as individuals—old,
middle-aged, young; meeting, parting, talking, walking, working. He is
never bored when alone in public places; the world's people are always
giving a show. He is also a close observer of people in more intimate situations; what movements do they make under the stress of such emotions as
anger, affection, enthusiasm, boredom?

Further assets of the choreographic personality are quite intangible,
and are noticeable more by their absence in a given piece of work than
by any test which could be devised for the would-be composer. One
of these is a dramatic sense, and an ability to grasp and hold an over-all
shape. This clearly calls for an emotional nature, responsive to dramatic
situation and development, whether this is expressed in an actual plot line
or in more abstract terms. Obviously, the calm, imperturbable person is
not fated to be much of a choreographer or, indeed, to be a performer either.
But this emotional personality must be firmly held in check by an objectivity
which is indispensable, which never allows feeling to run wildly undisci-
plined or to blur and dissipate the over-all shape. How many dances begin
with a stimulating idea, clothed in arresting movement, but then wander

and meander without climax, or point to a wavering conclusion—a mere stop, not an ending? There are individuals with talent who have an inborn sense of shape and dramatic contrast; those who lack this ability can be trained, I believe, to acquire it as part of the craft of choreography. Without it they are surely lost! Closely allied to this sense of shape is another intangible taste, which might be analyzed as a sense of fitness. This is the sense that stops vulgarity from creeping in, that prevents a mishmash of style, such as a sophisticated ballet lift in the middle of a primitive dance. This sense of fitness equally shuns the cliché, the *outré* and the sensational for their own sake; it unerringly knows the difference between valid theatricality and tricks. Can this be taught? Hardly. All evidence points to the fact that taste is a product of the total environment plus heredity, already so shot through with intangibles that one can only add a few oblique influences and hope for the best.

Among essentials which are not so ephemeral and which certainly can be taught are a good eye and a sensitive ear. The good eye knows how to choose the telling line, the right design—images gleaned from close observation and from that unknown quality, imagination, recur in profusion, so that there is little danger of running dry of ideas. Also, the well-trained ear is sensitive to music, hears the beat, the phrase, the harmony, the dynamics and melody plus the over-all "feel" of what the composer is saying. The choreographer is the sensitive and willing listener, but not the slave of the composer.

He should also be musically literate; know how music is organized on paper and be able to read a score with all its signs, marks, time signatures and note values; be knowledgeable about the history and literature of music, so as to have an informed opinion as to what to choose; be able to talk to any musician in his language, regardless of the fact that the musician probably knows little or nothing about dance or its vocabulary. In conferring with a composer, musical knowledge is particularly important for insuring clarity in the collaboration and for winning and holding the respect of the musician.

Two additional skills are extremely helpful, and might even make the difference between success and failure. One of these is facility, meaning speed, resourcefulness and judgment. The choreographer who is fast and bursting with ideas has a great advantage in the theater world, where time schedules are seldom generous. The stage is full of unhappy stories about dances which were not finished in time and frantic sessions with exhausted dancers whose choreographers were dawdlers or had a constitutional inability to make up their minds.

The other helpful quality is language skill. The choreographer who has a mind full of pungent, vivid or poetic language which he can use to convey his intentions is going to be much more inspiring and secure better co-operation from his dancers than the inarticulate one, who goes in for half sentences finished with a vague gesture. Language skill is for dances that have meaning; for those which are based only on physical movement, the vocabulary of a drill sergeant is quite sufficient.

Finally, our choreographer had better have something to say. This, to some young people, seems very formidable indeed, and they immediately search their souls for grandiose or cosmic themes which are not only unnecessary, but ill advised. Leave the massive themes to the older heads and hands; they are difficult enough even for the veterans. A young choreographer should choose something quite simple, which is thoroughly familiar or within the range of his own experience. There are many things to dance about within this apparently narrow scope, and also subjects which seem to me taboo. These will come up for consideration in a later chapter. For the time being it is important to emphasize that the main support of any subject matter a composer may choose is enthusiasm. The relationship of the creator to his theme is very much like that between lovers. He is intoxicated with its charms, embraces it on every possible occasion, dreams of it at night, delights in decking it out in the richest ornaments at his command. True to the history of lovers, there will be doldrums in the affair; the time will come when she frowns and is displeased with everything he says or does; and here, if the original passion was strong and fiery, a small spark will endure, and the despair will yield to a rekindling of the flame. The good choreographer is an ardent lover and suffused with enthusiasm for his new love, the next dance.

Having set forth what seem to me to be the characteristics of an ideal choreographer, I am struck by the comparison of this hypothetical creature with some of the highly successful choreographers of the day, many of whom display hardly a trace of the attitudes and skills on my list. From the evidence, it is obvious that a certain choreographer need not, for instance, care a fig about people; his extreme eminence in his profession does not depend on his conveying human feeling in his compositions, nor in even noticing that the dancers he is working with are people. Another composer has no musical feeling, yet he climbs into the higher brackets; while a third will use every cliché in the book and still succeed. But I have never heard of a choreographer who achieved even moderate success, who did not have a physical skill in moving bodies, and who was without an over-all theatrical sense of shape. These latter traits, then, seem to be the irreducible requirements for success in choreography, but are so meager a store of tools that an ambitious choreographer would be ill advised to content himself with so little.

Sources of Subject Matter—
What to Dance About?

3 Here it must be pointed out that the importance of subject matter is paramount mostly for the choreographer. It is his source, his dream, his love. For the audience it often makes very little difference what a dance is about; in fact, some of the most famous and successful dances in the world have been on trivial and inconsequential subjects. Consider "The Dying Swan." This, as performed originally by Anna Pavlova, has moved countless audiences to tears and remains the supreme example of romantic tragedy in dance. It is certainly not because of the actual subject. Who could care seriously about a swan, alive or dying? Only in so far as one can be pleased aesthetically by a handsome animal of any kind does the swan have an appeal. But there are no famous dances about the death of a noble horse or "The Dying Dog." So there must be other potent factors in such a dance. First there is the symbolic meaning, and then there is the movement. The swan glides, and this motion could be pleasingly imitated in dance in a period when grace and beauty were the sole aesthetic ideals. A four-footed animal moves by stepping, and the change of weight is accented, more jarring to the senses than the gliding movement of the bird. Then the swan has romantic proportions; it has the "swan neck," the long "s" curve which for centuries has been the symbol of beauty. There are other long-necked, graceful birds—the stork, for instance—but the poets swooned over the swan. No doubt this made the swan the aesthetic symbol of the period and the favorite ornament in the romantic pools and lakes of the nineteenth and early twentieth centuries. It was the final touch of elegant beauty to be seen in the vista of the garden from the drawing-room windows. Moreover, the swan would "stay put" and keep swimming around for the enjoyment of its owners. And what is so sad as the death of the supreme symbol of beauty? The poets of the day never tired of pointing out the lovely melancholy of expiring youth and grace; it was all so tragic and soulful. No wonder they invented a swan song for the dying swan. And this leads to the music for this particular dance. It, too, speaks to the emotions, with its wistful melody, played on the warmest of instruments, the cello. No real death agony here, just a fading away, with exquisite pathos and grace, in a romantic dusk. One final factor is the costume. Nothing could become the ballerina or epitomize the ethereal female more than the soft feathers, the dark jewel of the heart, the remote and pure whiteness of the whole contrasting with her raven-black hair. Lovely, mysterious, tragic. The genius of Michel Fokine conceived this symbol of the romantic age, embodying in one short solo all the most potent images of the then-current ideal. Now, the more sophisticated mid-twentieth-century mind does not respond so ecstatically to such a dance. Ideas have changed. Dying no longer seems so beautiful, and living more desirable. Still, the point to remember is that the subject per se was not important, except that it happened to be surrounded with supremely significant symbolism. (Would that choreographers of the day could do as well with contemporary subject matter!)

The insignificant theme need not be dependent on attached social values. A case in point is another famous dance, "Scheherazade," which still plays to S.R.O. whenever it is presented. Again, who could care about an Arabian Night's tale of intrigue in the harem? This is not going to give the businessman or the doctor anything to live with or think about. In fact, if he is sophisticated, the mishmash of pseudo-Arabian style and turn-of-the-century Russian taste is going to bore him. In its heyday, though, it was a sensation. It was exotic, colorful, sensuous. It was the supreme effulgence of the Russian Ballet for the dazzled world. The lesson here is that the remote, slight theme, if treated with freshness and originality, makes good theater dance, and again the subject is only the take-off point for the choreographer. This is not to say that dance cannot or should not deal with important subjects, but that it is not compelled to.

The blunt fact is that subject matter is mostly of concern to the choreographer, and whether it takes the form of narrative, symbolism or a conviction about style, is of no importance; the enthusiasm for it and innate talent is what keeps it alive, and puts it palpitating on the stage. Choreographers must resign themselves to the comparative indifference of the public to their subjects. What audiences see is mostly the result in movement, which is exciting or not, as the case may be. In drama much the same thing is apt to happen. I remember thinking that the plays "Waiting for Godot" and "The Chairs" were the two most depressing pieces of theater I ever saw in my life because of what they had to say, but I was astonished to find that many of my friends, and intelligent ones, too, hardly noticed what these plays were about, and considered them highly amusing and delightful because of their surface comedy. Nevertheless, the choreographer must behave as though the theme were of the highest significance, for if he does not, the fire goes out, the piece becomes routine and the public will know that nothing has happened when it is finally on view.

This realization leads to another rather grim revelation, which, among the arts, exists only in the dance. The subject which has suffused the choreographer with high enthusiasm may not, either at its roots of meaning or in its style of movement, please an audience or be comprehensible to it at all. The one inescapable condition surrounding the choreographer in his chosen art is the hard realism of "now." All other arts can wait for the verdict of history if they are rebuffed by the contemporary world—the choreographer not so. To keep faith with himself, he cannot pander to popular taste; he must choose his subject and the means to body it forth from his total convictions about values in art and life. If his work happens to be stimulating to audiences in their current state of development, he is very lucky indeed; but if not, he must resign himself to abandoning his dream child. Not for him the consolation of hanging his creation on the wall in all its original freshness, and waiting hopefully for perhaps post-humous appreciation. There must be hundreds, possibly thousands of dances—some of which were probably masterpieces—completely lost because of this tragic ephemerality. In contrast, one only has to think of painting and music, so often savagely rejected in their day, which a grateful world finally comes to accept and admire. This painful reality of the choreographer's "now" is a powerful temptation to abandon conviction and the most extreme flights of fancy in the interest of survival and prosperity. The wonder is that there are still so many choreographers who will not compromise, and who hug their ideals to their hearts in spite of failure and adversity.

The Independent Choreographer

The following section is directed primarily to independent choreographers, those who have a free hand and are at liberty to follow the dictates of their enthusiasms and convictions. Automatically ruled out are seventy-five per cent of those who are, or will be, engaged in choreographic tasks. These are the ones with jobs in the movies, television, shows, plays, operas, pageants, historical productions, commercial "spectaculars" and night clubs. The luxury of doing as they please is not for those hard-working and highly skilled directors, although the compensations in fame and money are dazzling indeed. Nevertheless, the taint of commercialism pervades them all in varying degrees, and the inevitable necessity for conforming to the demands of the situation damages the individuality of the choreographer and possibly prevents a contribution which might otherwise be more genuine and imaginative. I say "possibly prevents" because there are certain personalities who are at their best only in a given framework, and who feel most comfortable in a setting where they are told what to do. To these individuals freedom is a frightening specter, shunned and unloved. Also, of course, there are choreographers who have no ideas of their own.

For the others, then, who must decide for themselves what to dance about, there are some very serious points to consider. Being afire with ideas and enthusiasm, even if one is supported by technical know-how and good qualifications, is not going to be enough. Intelligence and selectivity in regard to the subject matter are not only desirable but imperative. I think we have to begin with an attempted assessment of something quite vague and difficult, the general climate of our time, which has a bearing on all behavior, including the feelings and predilections of choreographers There is a vast and compelling opinion expressed in countless ways in everyday living, which is so general that we are inclined to be as unconscious of it as we are of breathing. Yet this is the Great Influence, the voice of our time. If you agree with it, well and good, only be conscious of what the voice is saying. It would be fine indeed if audiences would listen to the voice as well, and come to a conclusion about it.

From the point of view of visual influences, it seems to me that architecture, especially for those who live in the city, speaks to us and for us with the most insistent cry. And what is it saying? Consider the modern city. A hodgepodge of style, a graveyard of early Victorian, Greek pillars, brownstones, neo-Gothic and what not. These are dead voices, however, and superimposed and dominant are the modern buildings—miles of them. Endless lines of steel and stone, square, hard, the perpendiculars stabbing the horizontals like enemies with spears, and no relief from the assault. The curve has all but vanished, and grace is now a sheet of green glass encased in an oblong of chromium—almost no landscaping, no sculpture, no ornament. The right angle is possibly the prime symbol of our age, eloquent of conflict. Its parent, the straight line, is thought to be best and smartest when it is shiny and naked, pointed slightly like the end of a weapon. The "clean line" is a cult. All this suggests force, too much steel and sterility and that other prime symbol, the fact. The right angle and the fact are the voices of our time. I am aware of the defense—real-estate costs, zoning laws, setback rules and economy in building materials, space and money. Nevertheless, underneath these shapes there must be a real need for and a belief in the hard, the practical and the violent, which has welled up from millions of demands by millions of people. In New York City, two particularly spectacular buildings are examples of the naked right angle —the Lever Brothers Building and the United Nations headquarters. The latter, a cold, icy slab with a bulbous tumor at its side, is unassuring as a house for the spirit of co-operation and brotherhood among the peoples of the world. The Lever Building is off balance, self-conscious, and, of course, naked and brutal. I am afraid this trend is world-wide, too, and cannot be laid at the door of "materialistic" America only.

Up-to-date interiors fare little better. Streamlined furniture offers rectilinear shapes to fit no anatomy except that of mechanical men, or else it swoops alarmingly in places where nobody should sag. So clean, though, with lines as naked as a scalpel.

All these streets and all these buildings are filled with people who are inoculated day after day with heavy visual doses of the right angle and massive amounts of fact, a delicious mixture, which makes them efficient and practical and sodden. Still, in spite of this, human beings dream, hope, pray, love, dance and sing. But the formal aspects of these things—religion, philosophy and art—so powerful in the past, are in eclipse and are unable to make any real impression on the visual symbols of the city. They are considered regressive and unimportant in an age which worships power and force.

In the extremely complex network of influences around us, I select architecture as an example of social attitudes and values only because it happens to impress me. Others might find verbal patterns or ideas more compelling. In any case, the connection between these things and dancing may seem very remote indeed, though this has not been my experience in teaching choreography. There is an inevitable relationship between the young dancer's store of the accumulated visual and mental patterns dominant in our age, and what he will come up with in composition. For example, he is likely to build a dance symmetrically, laying on each move with equal tension and plenty of physical force, and stop when the music gives out, without climax or point. This is rather like building a flat-topped brick wall that stops at the end of the property, and calling it a house. Or solving ten geometry problems. These are patterns of fact, and fact has nothing to do with choreography. Yet these forms, and others like them, are those with which general education has provided the dancer. Dance form is logical, but it is all in the realm of feeling, sensitivity and imagination, and these things have been pretty well beaten out of the average youth, as a positive hindrance to "getting on." How many children, full of buoyancy and talent as young painters, have been slowly squeezed into the regiment of fact, and have been turned into dry-as-dust academicians by the time they are fifteen? I find that young choreographers are all sensitive in only one way—they are terribly afraid of themselves. Suddenly, they are asked to abandon all their experience with practicality, and all the dance steps they have learned; to forget the years of docility and create from a basis of feeling. No wonder they feel naked and afraid.

I am not an advocate of "emoting" as the keystone to dance structure. It is well to say again that there is a discipline which must be followed in constructing dances. Just self-expression, provided that can be had at all, is certainly not acceptable. So to would-be choreographers I say: Look to see how far you have been inoculated with modern forms. If you are completely satisfied with the key shapes of our time, do not seek to compose. Human movements are not made of building blocks, nor with the right angle and the fact.

If the foregoing should seem to imply that I am going to propose a dreamy, emotional, soft kind of dancing, please be disabused at once. Certainly we must be strong, but strength is, to me, not just force, but rather a vocabulary of many means; not just an acceptance of current style, but an awareness of all shapes that may be expressive. This means that hardness and conflict must play a part in line, in form and in drama, but that their proper relation to other elements must be known and considered. Choreography is the search for and use of these elusive relationships. It begins with the most important step—the decision as to the basic idea from which the dance will spring. All else flows from this.

But first, I should say, the choreographer should try to come to a conclusion about his relationship to his time; in what respect does he agree with it, or where reject it? Does he want to sing along with the Voice or make music of his own? He has the privilege of being a conformist or a rebel. Also, of course, he can disagree with my analysis of the Voice entirely. All I ask is that he think about these things, and not merely coast along, unconscious of them all.

Where do ideas for dances come from? From many sources: experience from life itself, music, drama, legend, history, psychology, literature, ritual, religion, folklore, social conditions, fantasy; and from such vague prompt-ings as moods, impressions. And special interests, such as technical aspects of a theory of movement, comment on styles of dances or other arts, theatrical effects, or even abstract sources: line, color, shape, dynamics, rhythm. It is probably rare for a choreographer deliberately to make a choice of a theme by rational means. He is more likely to be seized by an enthu-siasm which wells up from the subconscious and demands to be born. All the thinking comes, or should, following the initial seizure, when decisions should be made by reason. Is this theme the kind of child who will make a dance—or should he be put out for adoption by an author, a painter or a psychologist? If he is to be mine, how shall he be clothed and educated and made to speak of my glorious vision? These considerations involve all the resources of choreographic craft.

For those who are interested in the process by which the thought or the theme arises in artists, there is a vast array of opinion on the matter, stretching over hundreds of years, and from many sources; one can delve into the area most sympathetic to him. Following are a few samplings from this material:

Aesthetics

Modern art is the annexation of forms by means of an inner pattern or scheme, which may or may not take the shape of objects, but of which, in any case, figures and objects are no more than the expression. The mod-ern artist's supreme aim is to subdue all things to his style, beginning with the simplest, least promising objects.

ANDRÉ MALRAUX

Physiology

Before an effective motor response is made, the great mass of incoming material undergoes a profound change. As the incoming impulses course toward the discriminating and organizing centers of the cortex, they are first delayed at the subcortical relay station, the thalmus. The reflex activity of the thalmus does not attain distinct consciousness, but nevertheless it contributes a feeling-tone to the awareness ultimately aroused.

MARGARET H'DOUBLER

Religion

The creative process is not constructive only, but has its destructive side, the nay no less than the yea; there is the dark and terrible aspect of God, the volcano as well as the Rock; creation comes from conflict.

P. W. MARTIN

Psychology

The transforming symbols indicating the living middle way between opposites are continually being produced by the deep unconscious; and the otherwise highly ambivalent autonomous complexes can, under suitable circumstances, be creatively integrated into the Self.

P. W. MARTIN

Philosophy

Everywhere in Creation we see ideas working which answer more or less to those within ourselves; and it is this answering of one to the other, of the outer to the inner, which forms the very ground of all science and art, and the joy that we feel in Truth and Beauty.

EDWARD CARPENTER

Let us say that the mysterious and complex process by which the artist is motivated has been completed and that the theme has said to him, "Arise, I am come." At this point, the choreographer should take himself firmly in hand and proceed to a close and reasoned look at the lovely thing which has thrown him into a fevered state. So easy to say and so difficult to do! This is like advising the lovesick to consider the imperfections of his beloved before plunging headlong into marriage; he can't and he won't! However, if we all keep insisting on more reason in both love and choreography at this fateful point, some caution may lodge in a cranny here and there and prevent heartbreaking mistakes from occurring.

The Theme

4 No matter what the subject, the first test to apply is in one word—action. Does the theme have inherently the motivation for movement? At all times we must be aware that the dance art is unique in its medium of movement (along with mime, a sister art). Unique, too, is its power to evoke emotion within its vocabulary, to arouse the kinetic sense, to speak of the subtleties of the body and the soul. But the language has definite limitations and should not be forced to communicate beyond its range, which is, again, that part of experience which can be expressed in physical action. Rather than generalize too much on what subject matter is or is not suitable, let us go to some concrete examples, culled from choices already made by modern dance choreographers:

"Etiquette" (Emily Post)

"Remorse"

"Vivacity"

"Soliloquy in the Morning"

"Roads to Hell"

"Yerma" (after Lorca)

"The Braggart"

"The Lonely Ones" (after Steig)

"Ruins and Visions"

"Let's Build a Town"

"Flickers" (early movies)

"Timely Ballads"

"Fables for Our Time"
    (after Thurber)

"The Shakers"

"Prairie"

"As I Lay Dying" (after Faulkner)

"Petulance"

"Politeness"

"Fright"

"Blues in the Night"

"To One Dead"

"The Exiles"

"Ceremony of Innocence"

"La Malinche" (Mexican legend)

"Rites"

"How Long Brethren?"
    (Negro songs of protest)

"The Emperor Jones" (after O'Neill)

"Goodbye to Richmond"

"Folk-Say" (after Sandburg)

"The Big City"

"Dawn in New York" (after Lorca)

All the above dances pass the first test—that is, for action. Movement is inherent in their structure, flows naturally from the sources of human behavior; consequently they do not "run dry," nor do they have to depend on contrived passages to keep them alive. Or, to put it conversely, none of these themes would be better in a book on psychology (i.e. more meaningful to the senses), or as legend, or as folklore or literature. I also mean by action that the dance must bring some revelation, some comment, some added shade of meaning to a theme, which cannot be found in its original state. If it does not achieve this, it simply is not worth doing. All these themes are in the dramatic area, and have a very wide scope indeed. Some are elaborate, with plot and subplot; others are very simple, reduced to a mood, and performed by a solo dancer. Selected from the hundreds of themes in the last thirty years, these are a few which have been danced, ranging from the slight to the heroic. In even such a brief list there is a striking range in sources of material, and all of it valid. Three dances spring from Spanish soil, but they do not employ Spanish movement. There are many based on single aspects of behavior, such as "The Braggart" and "Fright." Six are from literature; three use words in the dance itself. Two religious themes appear: "The Exiles," taken from the Biblical account of Adam and Eve, and "The Shakers." There are also four comedies; two using folk material; three on city and country ideas; one using history, "Goodbye to Richmond"; and one, "Blues in the Night," which could be called ethnic. Just a mere listing of the names of the dances indicates how subject matter has changed or widened, as nothing like these titles was used in the nineteenth century or before.

Conversely, here are a few examples of static ideas in dramatic themes which would be difficult or impossible to treat, because they have no inherent action:

> "A young man, exhausted, admires the vitality of nature, the sheen on the leaves, the full fruit, the vigor of a cock in the barnyard."

This is a fragment of a long script. How are we going to do this scene? The only human being in it has no action—he's exhausted. And what shall we do for a cock—use a stuffed one, or a dancer dressed up as a bird?

Ballads and folk songs are enticing. For instance, the tragic song of Lord Randal and his mother:

> "What have you been drinking, my own darling son?
> What have you been drinking, my own darling one?"

"A cup of cool poison, mother, make my bed soon,
  For I'm sick to my heart, and I fain would lie doon."
"What'll you will to your mother, my darling son?"
"My house and my farm, mother; make my bed soon,
  For I'm sick to my heart, and I fain would lie doon."

"What'll you will to your wife, my own darling one?"
"The great keys of hell, mother, make my bed soon,
  For I'm sick to my heart and I fain would lie doon."

This is touching, dramatic and has a haunting melody, but movement is missing. The drama is all in the implications of the words.

"Two men in a prison see a bird outside their small window. They discuss the drab security of their lives, contrasted to the dangerous freedom of the bird."

You cannot philosophize in dance. This is for words, or possibly a combination of words and movement. In certain cases the sum total of the dance may suggest a philosophic content, but this would only be implied.

Refreshingly absent from the list on page 34 are a number of suspect themes; I will not say that they are impossible to use, but that they should be approached with extreme caution:

Propaganda

The idea of social reform, class struggle or whatever it is, can overwhelm the dance when nothing counts so much as the message. This is usually better from a speaker's platform or in a book, because we have strayed into the world of fact. A statistic is not a good subject for a dance, no matter how emotional the composer might feel about it.

Cosmic Themes

The Creation of the World, the Music of the Spheres, War, the Labors of Hercules, the Industrial Revolution, and grandiose ideas of this sort are, in my opinion, out of bounds. Movement is not the medium in which to tell these things; the scale is too vast. Only by pinpointing some incident connected with the idea could a suggestion of the whole be made.

Mechanical Themes

Fortunately, there is a waning tendency today to dance like the machine. Seldom do we see a "ballet mécanique." Still, there are influences at work to persuade the dancer to explore this field, not so much to imitate wheels, piston rods and the assembly line, as to produce mechanical movement. We are told that the body is a wonderful machine, and so it is, in part. This leads to an absorption with body mechanics and finally to an obsession with technique which loses sight of the objective: the communication of the human spirit. A really virtuoso technique is very exciting, but also very rare. Most technical dances are just mechanical. I think the age of the machine which flies faster than sound and operates with a hair's-breadth precision has been a great factor in producing dances which are examples of physical skill and little else.

Literary Themes

There are elements in literature which cannot be translated into dance. Language can give us facts, situations, relationships and states of being which are very difficult for the art of movement alone to tell. You cannot say in dance, "This is my mother-in-law," unless there is a careful sequence leading to such a statement. It would have to be established in three relationships: mother-girl, husband-girl, mother-in-law-husband. But words have said it all in two seconds. Conversely, a character and behavior delineation which would take the author pages to complete might be done in seconds by the dancer. These time differences represent pitfalls in resorting to literary themes, especially in poetry. And there are others. Some key ideas—assuming that they are important—cannot be stated at all. For example, suppose we are going to make a dance-drama out of the story of Jephthah's daughter. The tragedy lies in Jephthah's vow to kill the first creature who meets him on his return if God will help him defeat the enemy. One could not depend on more than ten per cent of an audience remembering the story, or dutifully looking at a program note. So, left to movement alone, we would see Jephthah praying earnestly in one scene, and meeting his daughter with a sword in the next. Even if there were a full battle scene, showing Jephthah victorious, this would be confusing. Dilemmas of this kind have been solved by using a narrator, and making frank use of the text, but this is not a favorite device, and is very difficult to deal with, besides. I shall have more to say about the combining of words and movement in a later chapter.

Then there is the very literary and condensed use of ideas one finds in much modern poetry; it is full of the symbolism of things, an imagery which the dance cannot use; beautifully suited to its own medium, but quite unsuited to the dance. The following is an excerpt from a poem by Malcolm Brinnin, "Death of This Death":

> Praise then the young whose cloudless willing hands
> Blueprint a shoal of cities, dare to turn
> From rotting acres of the dispossessed
> To meet life's penalty. Their maps define
> The possible dominion of the free,
> A calm community
> That, flowering in the culture of decay,
> Turns death to seed within our living day.

The general idea could be danced, the young forming a better life out of the chaos of the old, but the images are far from the realm of the dance. "A shoal of cities," "rotting acres," "a calm community" are images that suggest no movement. Moreover, each line has the characteristic fast timing of the word; the picture changes approximately every two seconds. In poetry, this is stimulating; in dance, it would be futile and frantic.

Two more warnings about literature. Since potential choreographers are widely read and susceptible to the delights of the word in a word-dominated age, they are apt to fall under the spell of—just words.

A good example is an excerpt from Theodore Roethke's "The Lost Son":

> Rich me cherries a fondling's kiss
> The summer bumps of ha?
> Hand me a feather, I'll fan you warm,
> I'm happy with my paws.

This could be fun, and there is certainly a place for nonsense. But again, literary fun is not likely to be translatable. We must look for comedy in terms of what is comprehensible in movement.

Incidentally, a word about the naming of dances. Choreographers can be incomprehensible just in their titles, which, without program notes, are expected to convey the whole meaning of the dance. It is scarcely fair to audiences to present something called "Seed of the Unseen," followed by "Wind of the Unknown," and leave them to flounder. This would be the result of a horror of the obvious, reading too much impressionistic literature, or possibly a lazy indifference to the precise.

One other kind of theme to try to avoid is the too-complex scenario. Without words that are clues to character and situations in a drama, we can't be expected to remember long scenarios. The following, called "Icarus," would be an example. Read it through once and try to repeat it from memory.

> Phaedra and Ariadne, watching for Icarus's return, are warned by the herald of the Athenian ship approaching with the sacred victims of the Minotaur. A group of Cretans also come to watch and one of them has a vision of impending death. Theseus, arriving with the Athenians, is greeted by ceremonial runners from the court of Minos, and he relates to Minos and the Cretans the story of the miraculous winged creature which the Athenians saw from their ship, and their horror as they saw him, suddenly encircled by lightning, fall headlong into the sea. Theseus concludes the narration by disclosing the body to them. Erigone enters and laments the death of her son. The concluding chorus invokes glory to him who dares, a paean for heroes.

There are further pitfalls in the literary-dramatic theme. Modern choreographers are attracted to intensely emotional situations in plays and legends and mythology, which are often valid as dance material (i.e., they contain action possibilities), but which the composer mutilates so completely that the theme becomes emasculated and meaningless. Consider, as an example, what happens when a young choreographer reads of Phaedra, either in the play or in the original legend, and decides that this is a tragic role after her own heart. She is not going to bother with all the characters. She has no men to work with, and all those people are unnecessary anyway. Besides, she is looking for a solo role. So she makes the dance out of Phaedra's climactic agony, using her serving woman as a foil. Now, not one spectator in a thousand will remember what "Phaedra" is all about, and the choreographer neglects to explain the plot even in a program note, so what the curtain reveals is two young women agonizing for ten minutes or so, for an unknown reason. Nobody could care about the spectacle, unless the chief dancer had some extraordinary movement to offer, a dazzling personality, or other absorbing values extraneous to the plot. These extra ingredients are not likely to be present in nine cases out of ten.

I think this error in judgment arises from a fundamental misconception or ignorance about the basic reactions of human nature, and what relation the theater has to them. Fundamentally, we are repelled by tragedy and suffering and are attracted to the bright and the pleasant. Who would not automatically prefer a charming gathering of congenial friends to a trip through an insane asylum? I am speaking of the normal human being, not of the subhuman species which delights in seeing Gestapo torture, or witches burned at the stake. There has always been the morbid element in society, but these people demand real blood, the actual pound of flesh, and you will never find them at a dance concert, battening on the play-acting of two young ladies who feel desperate about something.

The tragic theme, nevertheless, is eminently suitable for dance, but— and it is a big "but" which choreographers forget at their peril—our fundamental aversion to the depressing situation must be changed to sympathy and compassion. This is achieved by showing causes and motivation, and these must be bodied forth before our eyes—not just in program notes or poetic quotations about the subject, but in flesh and blood movement. Many choreographers who snip out scenes from plays have not learned the first thing about drama, which every playwright knows and is at great pains to employ: that careful character delineation and motivation make the play. There is an appalling amount of vague mourning and agonizing going on in the modern-dance field. Dancers love to suffer, and while they wallow in tragedy, they alienate and bore their audiences.

If the theme is a happy one, none of the above considerations need apply. We automatically like gay, pleasant people and things, and nobody has to be induced into a receptive state to enjoy them.

About subject matter in brief: the theme is likely to arrive spontaneously from the total experience of the composer; it should then be closely examined for action possibilities and general suitability. If it is a "dark" theme, the treatment must differ from that of a "light" one. All possible knowledge about the craft of choreography should then be brought to bear in the creative process, in matters of movement and form, and an equal amount of care should be devoted to the supporting factors.

Music, costuming, sets, props, lighting, the title and program notes are primary ones. For the dance, like all theater arts, is a synthesis, and the proper blending of the elements is the responsibility of the choreographer. But at the core of it all is the dance itself, which now, in the twentieth century, has a body of theory about composition to help and support the choreographer. All composers, both young and experienced, would do well to inquire into the craftsmanship of choreography.

Two

THE CRAFT

The Ingredients and the Tools

5 At the point when the subject is chosen and the opportunity or necessity for composing is at hand, I imagine that ninety per cent of potential or experienced choreographers plunge into creating with whatever background in technique or performing they have been able to acquire, and very little knowledge of the ingredients, the tools, or the know-how of building dances. Choreographic theory is still so new and so sparsely taught, that it is simply not available to many, and also, underlying the whole subject, is the attitude that the ability to compose is somehow heaven-sent and that inspiration is damaged by the cold hand of thought and analysis. This certainly springs from the layman's antiquated point of view about artists: that they are strange, dreamy people who live alone in garrets and produce masterpieces by some dark mysterious process that comes on them like a clap of thunder. Many a flattered set of parents have been shocked to find that their beloved child, who is proclaimed talented by his teachers, is not going to leap to fame and fortune overnight by "inspiration," but is going to have to have years of expensive training. These shocks no longer occur so frequently in such arts as music and painting, because the necessity for learning how to compose in these is so well known. Dancing has not reached this stage yet, even among the dancers themselves, and it seems to me it is an area in which the dance is most backward. One can only state the case for choreography and hope that time will prove the value of it.

Long ago, in dealing with the people who came to me for help in composing, I discovered that they were far from prepared to construct a finished piece of work. They were good technicians, rather like men who have been taught to run a complicated piece of machinery, the purpose of which they have no idea. Does it make cloth or buttons or colored crayons? All they know is that it runs magnificently and is a joy to operate. The gears mesh smoothly, the wheels turn, and all they think they want to learn is to alter the design slightly, so that it will sell as a new model. And surely it must be constructed to make something worth while? Yes, indeed, but only if they know the right materials to put into it, and how to adjust the gears to make the desired product.

To drop the simile, the student knows nothing about the meaning of the movements he has so laboriously acquired, nor how they may be put to use. Therefore, the major part of his studies with me is first of all devoted to a detailed inquiry into the ingredients of a dance, how they may be understood and used purposefully. Only then are considerations of form, construction and real choreography undertaken.

I first warn the students that habitual sequences studied in technique classes had better be abandoned for the time being, as these will be useful only after their meanings are understood. The purpose of the class is to find new movement, which we will undertake to discover on the basis of principle. This is, to begin with, quite frightening, I am sure—rather like abandoning the dear familiar homeland and putting out to sea without a compass. Also the students know very well that hundreds of dances have been made on the basis of recombining well-known steps, but this, they are dimly aware, is arranging and not creating. One of the famous definitions of choreography is "the arranging of steps in all directions." But we are going to set about the problem in a different way and from a different direction, which will lead to composing and not arranging.

All the clues for this theory come from life itself. Every movement made by a human being, and far back of that, in the animal kingdom, too, has a design in space; a relationship to other objects in both time and space; an energy flow, which we will call dynamics; and a rhythm. Movements are made for a complete array of reasons involuntary or voluntary, physical, psychical, emotional or instinctive—which we will lump all together and call motivation. Without a motivation, no movement would be made at all. So, with a simple analysis of movement in general, we are provided with the basis for dance, which is movement brought to the point of fine art. The four elements of dance movement are, therefore, design, dynamics, rhythm and motivation. These are the raw materials which make a dance, and so fundamental are they that, without a balanced infusion of each, the dance is likely to be weakened, and without any two of them it will be seriously impaired. To be sure, all four parts of movement will be there in some degree no matter what is done, but to use them skillfully, so that all the mutations are understood and can be intelligently chosen to support the idea, takes quite a lot of study.

So now the student is called upon to think in terms of elements rather than steps. To plunge him into the stream immediately, I ask for a study which will cope with all four at once in what I call "bite-size" choreography. In only one measure of four/four time I ask for, first, a motivation which is realized in movement, with at least two contrasts in design, in dynamics, in rhythm. This may seem quite formidable on paper, but I have had hundreds of students who could do it well and none who failed to grasp it; and no two of them ever did it alike. These one-bar phrases are arranged in various directions in the framework of a simple form, at the end of which the student has nine of these measures, which might loosely be compared to single words, like nouns in language. Nine "words" is quite a vocabulary in the dance, and if the student knows how to complete them with syntax, grammar and phrasing, he will have quite enough movement to complete a whole dance. Their main value, however, is to provide a small pattern in which these four elements of movement can be clearly seen and remembered. The value of the contrasts is pointed out again and again—in experiments in which these are removed. For instance, the student is asked to eliminate all sharp dynamics and do the same movements all smooth. Immediately it is apparent to everybody that many repetitions of the all-smooth bar very quickly become boring. This is true of all the elements. The evenly spaced rhythm is too monotonous; it needs the contrast of unevenness to keep it stimulating. Similarly, the design which has no contrast is dull. I am well aware that this emphasis on contrast is born of Western culture; perhaps it is even particularly American. The adventurousness and restless spirit of a still-young nation certainly permeates almost everything about us; we are notorious for being less leisurely than most other peoples in our ways, and more demanding of variety. The doctrine of much contrast would be alien to the ethos of Asiatic culture, which has quite other values, and not so important even to the rest of the Western world. So I must say that this idea, introduced at the beginning of choreographic training, seems valuable particularly for American dancers. Nevertheless, I have had many foreign students in my classes, and those whose background is ethnic or ballet have derived considerable benefit from this theory, which, although originated by a modern American dancer, is not tied to that technique or only to that country.

To get back to one-bar phrases, I deliberately chose them because they are easy to do, just stimulating enough to be interesting; they somewhat allay the fears of the novice about the word choreography, which sounds forbidding and full of intellectual terrors; and particularly because they capture at once the essence of the four elements which the student must learn to deal with as his basic materials. Thinking in these terms about dancing is likely to be quite difficult and challenging at first. The student has come from years of explicit instruction in the use of muscles, co-ordination, balance, centering, correct "line"; he has learned lots and lots of "steps" or sequences, and has been thoroughly disciplined in the right way to do these things by hundreds of corrections. It is very rare for him to have any freedom whatever from strict instruction in the "way." Time out for improvisation in technical courses for professional dancing is almost unknown, and only partially operates in the teaching of children or nonprofessional adults. Consequently, the choreographic student finds it quite bewildering to be presented with so much freedom and in fact to be specifically cut loose from his former vocabulary. One more familiar companion of all these years is also temporarily denied him —music. The stimulating sound which helps him feel like dancing is reduced to a bare minimum while he is asked to concentrate on the elements of movement. With this bird's-eye view, so to speak, of his new domain in terms of the four elements, he is then led to examine them one by one at closer range and in considerable detail.

Assignment

Bring nine one-bar phrases. These consist of three sets: the first, walking; the second, running and jumping; the third, hopping steps combined with others. Each set is in the same three directions, forward diagonal, from up right to down left; sideways, from left to right; and around, the body revolving counterclockwise. A short coda may be arranged to finish each of these sets for exhibition purposes. Each bar is to have a motivation and contrasts in design, dynamics and rhythm; and is to be repeated by students in single file as many times as necessary to traverse the existing space.

Design, Part 1

SYMMETRY AND ASYMMETRY

6 The design section of the craft is by far the most extensive of any of the parts. First of all, it must be clearly understood that dance is an art in which design has two aspects: time and space. We can speak of design in the sense of static line. That is, a dance can be stopped at any moment and it will have a design in space. Also it can have still moments that are like photographs or drawings. In addition, there is the design in time, which exists through any moving sequence, lasting from a few seconds to a full-length dance. This is much more complex than the single-space design, and ranges from a simple transition of one movement to another —which forms a relationship in time and therefore has a shape—to the lengthier phrase-shape, and finally to the over-all structure, which can be compared to form in drama, music and literature. It is much more difficult to perceive the design in time than in space. The eye must remember how movements follow each other, and this takes practice and training. Lay audiences probably do not remember a fraction of the time design of a dance, and few professional dancers do either. Nevertheless, there is such an innate sense of structure in most people that they usually know unerringly whether the form is good or not. The ones who must really understand and remember design in time, and know why it is good or bad, are the choreographers.

The innate sense of structure in people has been acquired through thousands of experiences with design. Every day in every life, the senses are impressed with the shape of objects, from the humble comb and brush to huge architectural designs or natural phenomena, like mountains; with pictures in magazines, newspapers, books, movies, television; with the figures of people, their faces, their clothes and automobiles; with ideas, from the sports page to the sermon, and the language they are encased in. One can hardly list all the battery of design with which the everyday life is confronted, so infinite is it. Now, there is a conscious or unconscious reaction to each one of these things, which is further complicated by individual differences in taste, education and environment. Some people love the juke-box-designed music and loathe "long-hair stuff." Discrimination and judgment are operating constantly, deciding what is agreeable and what is not. There are also changes from time to time in what the individual likes, through his exposure to new experiences. Not only is it impossible to lump classes of people together and declare, for instance, that all bankers like Rodgers and Hammerstein musicals, but the taxi driver who has been neatly pigeonholed as a man who always has baseball tuned in on his radio, will be found one day to be listening to nothing but Verdi.

Underneath all this maze of divergence in taste, I think I can discern a few constants and some fairly large areas of agreement as to the impact and meaning of design. If the choreographer knows what the basic reactions of people are in these areas, he should be able to make use of them to strengthen the dance design, because he will then be using not merely the design or style of the day, or the fad of a specialized class, but a much more solid underlying shape-sense. In describing these constants, it must be understood that I am referring primarily to reactions of the Western world.

I think of design in general as falling into two major categories, symmetrical and asymmetrical, each of which may be of two kinds, oppositional or successional. Consider the meaning of symmetry first. Symmetry always suggests stability, but is subject to gradations of this feeling according to the purpose which it serves. The armchair promises comfort and support for the symmetrically formed human body; the door is a reassuring framework to go through for the same reason; the Arch of Triumph is a grandiose symmetrical structure inspiring courage and pride in the solid achievements of a country (how disconcerting if it were full of knobs and asymmetrical quirks); a Christopher Wren church rises serenely to God with a promise of spiritual safety. There are thousands of balanced designs, some to serve symmetrically proportioned people; some from an emotional demand for balance and security; some to fulfill a function, such as a car; but all making an indelible connection in the mind of man between symmetry and stability. But when people leave these appropriate designs for living, and enter the world of aesthetics, the demands and the values are completely reversed. No longer do they want security, comfort, repose. Art is for stimulation, excitement, adventure. Painters know very well that this calls for asymmetry. So do sculptors and musicians. Choreographers are apt to use too much symmetry, however, for reasons which are stated elsewhere, and this will spell monotony and death for a dance. If audiences were looking for a soothing, unexciting evening, the chances are they would rather be home in their armchairs, drowsing beside their symmetrical fireplaces. This is not to say that symmetry has no function in dance. The movement art, like others, must have moments of rest and repose, which are often more satisfying when symmetrically designed. Also, absolute balance of parts has its uses at the beginning of a sequence, to indicate a serenity of spirit before desire has begun, or again at an ending, when some dénouement of peace or conviction is to be stated. (See pages 52–53 for designs for one body; pages 54–55 for designs for two bodies.)

Here, speaking as a choreographer, I should like to diverge from the main theme briefly to lodge a small protest against some tendencies in theater design. Doubtless this text will never meet the eye of an architect, so I shall consider it just another point in the discussion of the two kinds of design. A theater is a functional place, one part of which is for doing, and the other for receiving. The doing part should provide every technical device in structure and equipment for whatever kind of art it is to contain. Although this seems obvious, there are many theaters which do not have properly equipped stages and backstage areas for drama and dance. There are plenty of them with no crossovers at all, and I know of at least one with all the dressing rooms two flights up a spiral staircase and no elevator! However, these mild eccentricities are not alarming, only inconvenient. What I have in mind particularly are some of the new ideas used in designing the viewing parts of the theater. There is a tendency to treat these like works of art in themselves, with elaborate decoration and the asymmetry of a painting. This turns the house into a place of stimulation and excitement; it becomes a show in itself, and it seems to me that this is not the function of it. One theater I have seen has S-shaped aisles set at an angle; a balcony which swoops down to one side; montage murals on the walk, with eccentric designs which are so complicated as to claim prolonged attention. Put very simply, it seems to me that the show should be on the stage, that the house should be a pleasant place designed for comfort, easy sitting and seeing, symmetrically calm, friendly and warm in its color and decoration, and presenting no out-and-out competition to the stage. There was some excuse for the elaborately

SYMMETRY

ASYMMETRY

Opposition

SYMMETRY

ASYMMETRY

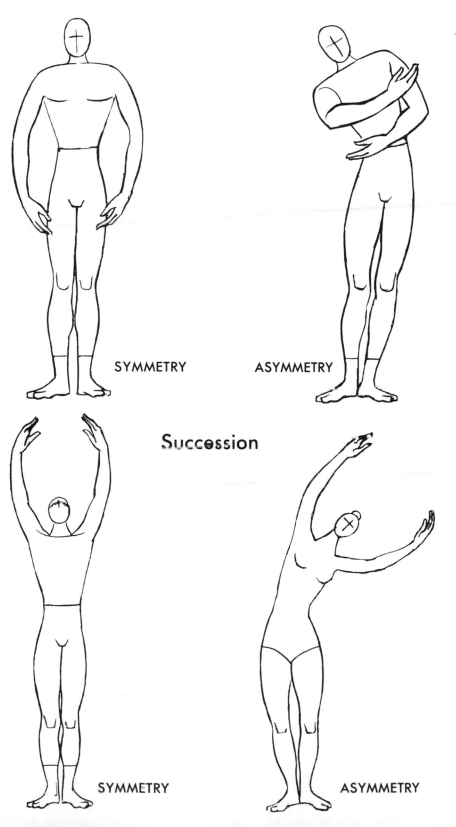

SYMMETRY ASYMMETRY

Succession

SYMMETRY ASYMMETRY

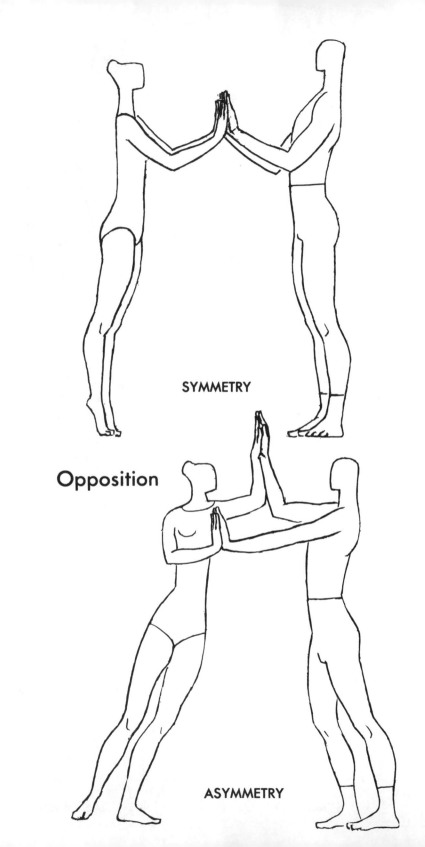

SYMMETRY

Opposition

ASYMMETRY

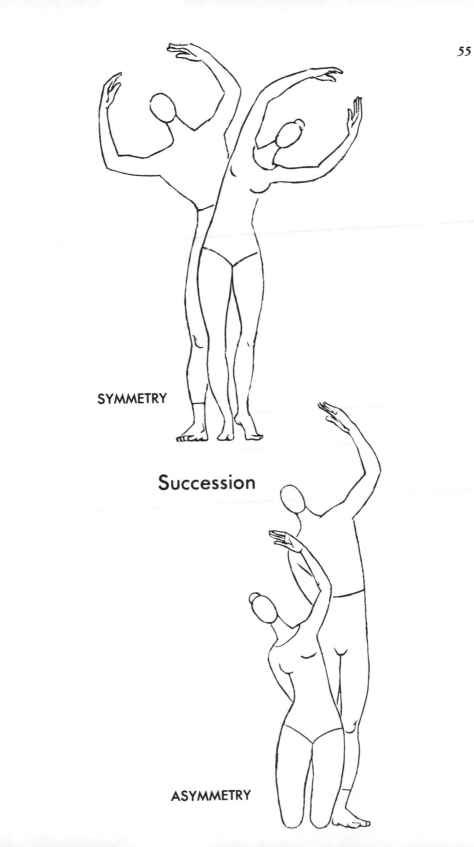

SYMMETRY

Succession

ASYMMETRY

decorated theaters patterned after the halls of palaces in a bygone age, when royalty set the style for all social events, but such places, though dazzling, seem inappropriate for our democratic and functional theater of today—an anachronism, in fact.

If symmetry should be used sparingly in choreography because of its calming effect, then asymmetry, which stimulates the senses, is the area to court and understand for dancing. People have no less fundamental reactions to this than to symmetry, again gained through thousands of associations in everyday living, which they bring to the theater. For instance, large numbers of people can hardly avoid being exposed to the design of contests, all asymmetrical and exciting, whether in sports, politics, wars, business or whatever. The unpredictability of the contest, and the imbalance in which the weight of the outcome swings now this way and now that—leaving aside the emotional involvement—make a major impression of an uneven pattern on everybody—and they will find this design stimulating wherever it occurs. This is probably largely unconscious, but it seems to be there nevertheless. Utopian schemes for a perfectly balanced society in which all the horrid competition has been eliminated, in which everything is evenly proportioned and unpredictability is ruled out, have often foundered on the rock of boredom. Security is essential for human happiness in some things, but in everything, no. Nietzsche stated this long ago in his analysis of Greek society. He saw clearly that the Greek ideal of moderation and balance in all things was Apollonian, but that they very wisely provided an escape from this monotony in their Dionysian rites. There lived within the Apollonian man a Dionysus, an unquenchable desire for excitement in breaking all the rules, indulging in the passion for unevenness—and freedom from rational balance. The dance is an experience from which excitement is demanded, and in this sense it is Dionysian.

Of the thousands of smaller examples from life which might be used to illustrate this point, here are a few: We do not care for the public speaker who runs on in a monotone of logical thought put into carefully constructed sentences; we prefer some passion in such a man (juttings out from the plane of the horizontal) and, if possible, some wit (unexpected unevenness). The strictly symmetrical landscaping of gardens and parks is not in favor in this day; the regimenting of nature makes her look very dead indeed, and provides no charm (stimulation). The bunch of flowers is carefully arranged unevenly, although the vase for holding it is reassuringly symmetrical. A sure-fire touch of humor is provided by the young man who arrives to see his lady love with a bunch of flowers wired into a stiff, pincushion shape. What we most admire in nature is her waywardness. There is absolutely no symmetry about her, and, although I have heard of one plant which has an evenly four-sided stem, I doubt if it always grows in a strict perpendicular, so it can be ruled out as a slight aberration.

The theater and the concert hall are places where we like and expect excitement and asymmetrical design. This can be more concretely dealt with, in visible terms, in the dance than in music and drama. The actor cannot very well hold his body in complex off-balance designs while in the surge of a scene, nor should he, because the drama is in the words, backed up by believable and fairly natural movements of a human being. But dance can take off into flights of symbolism in which highly stylized, designed movement can speak convincingly of emotional states without any connection with realism. I affirm that this is at least partly true because the receiver is able to "read" the movement accurately through his awareness of the basic meanings of design. For example, an actor is playing a scene in which he is tormented by conflicting desires; this is accompanied by some "business," pacing up and down, and various gestures having to do with the natural movements people make in such situations. The dancer can make these movements, too, though they must be put through a process which removes them from pantomine. He also has in his potential vocabulary designed conflicts which can make use of all parts of the body in thousands of combinations and in all directions, heights and depths, in all dynamics and in all rhythms. To express conflict, these movements must be asymmetrical, with only an occasional balanced design if a rest is needed. Of all the four parts of movement, the design, especially that in space, will most quickly tell of the intention, the mood and the meaning.

Within these two major divisions of design—symmetry and asymmetry—are two subdivisions. Any of these major patterns is either oppositional or successional. By this I mean that their lines are either opposed, in a right angle, or are flowing, as in a curve. These two design elements have an exactly opposite effect on the eye, and are of great importance in the understanding of choreography. Opposed lines always suggest force; energy moving in two directions dramatizes and emphasizes the very idea of energy and vitality. The closer the opposition comes to a right angle, the more power is suggested. The more the angle is narrowed, the weaker it becomes. Were the ideal in dancing to be as strong as possible, then the best dance would be done in nothing but asymmetrical right-angle designs, indicating maximum power (in the right angle) and maximum excitement (in the asymmetry). This, of course, would be a colossal bore. As a matter of fact, something close to this was tried as a vocabulary in the early days of modern dance, but fortunately it was soon abandoned in favor of a more comprehensive eloquence. The oppositional design strengthens and fortifies any mood or meaning which calls for aggressive energy and vitality. It is indispensable for any idea of conflict, either emotional and subjective or with some outside person or force. But it is also useful for happier expressions of energy, as in an exuberant joyousness, or an exultant hope. Contrary to this is the successional design, which is always milder and gentler. Whether in curves or straight lines, the unobstructed linear shape, which flows pleasantly along its comfortable paths, offers no resistance to the eye. The most soothing design, therefore, is a symmetrical one with a successional pattern. Considerably more stimulating is the asymmetrical succession, which is the area of grace and beauty; here there is just enough asymmetry to provide a pleasant alertness, with neither oppositional shocks, on the one hand, nor the deadly balance of symmetry, on the other. These two kinds of body organization bear a further suggestion of meaning. The contrasted-energy design, opposition, seems always to retain some or all of its power, no matter how much the lines extend outward from the body. The crossing of the energy directions seems to anchor, or imprison, some of the force, so that not all of it escapes into space. The body still looks energized. Not so with the successional design. Here the energy necessary to make the movement seems to flow along the paths of the body, like electricity through a wire, and escapes through whatever terminal the eye is led to. Unless energized by another flow, the body remains a passive instrument without a sense of force of its own. Of course, if the energy injections are rapid enough so that one flow scarcely dies before another is begun, there is a continuous impression of energy being expanded, but all of it is escaping from the body, so that the dancer does not seem to be "doing" with his strength, but appears to be played upon by a force which goes through him.

All the above observations are of oppositions and successions as found with their natural meanings, so to speak. It seems obvious that the choreographer should use their potentialities to strengthen whatever his idea calls for. But it must be pointed out that one of the other elements could be so applied to design as to weaken its natural effect. For instance, a strong oppositional design could be done with such a slow effortless legato that its natural force would be almost completely dissipated. It is conceivable that one might wish this very effect, but without understanding these matters the choreographer might fall (and has) into such a passage inadvertently. Conversely, the most determined and stabbing effort to look strong or angry or combative with the use of successional design is not going to be nearly as convincing as it would be if oppositions were used; the wrong design has weakened the idea.

Assignment

To realize these ideas, the student is asked to bring in space designs for the single body. That is, he is to prepare several symmetricals and asymmetricals, both in oppositions and successions which do not move in space or time (except for the simplest transitions from one to the other) and are not motivated, but are merely exercises for the manipulation of line, in order to become familiar with the ideas of their organization.

Design, Part 2

FOR ONE AND MORE BODIES

7 With a conception of the natural implications of design established, we now undertake to put them in the service of an idea. That is, designs are chosen which will accurately convey an attitude to some human activity or feeling. Students are given themes to work with, single ideas, which are neutral, so to speak; capable of various interpretations; and grouped into a loose pattern which gives them some continuity. Among those I have found successful are (to paraphrase William Blake):

> Think in the morning,
> Work in the noon,
> Eat in the evening,
> In the night, rest.

> or Waiting
> Realization
> Conclusion

> or Coming
> Meeting
> Parting

In beginning to work on any of these, the student is first asked to decide on an attitude to the idea. Suppose the idea is "waiting." This can be done with fear, anxiety, impatience, stoicism, boredom, hope, pleasure, resentment, and in many other ways. It could be further complicated by who is doing the waiting—a child, a grandmother or a young girl—and also what is waited for—a person, an event, or an inner change such as a realization of misfortune or good luck. For the time being, however, these are omitted; choosing a design on a simple basis is difficult enough. The student, therefore, is expected to be himself, the age and sex he is, and to be awaiting some exterior event. One of the first things that confronts him is the fact that the natural positions people assume under different emotions are very unreliable guides to the way they feel. For instance, in anxiety, people may very well sit back in a chair, close their eyes and clasp their hands quietly, all in symmetrical design. This will never do for the visual art of the dance. The turmoil of emotion going on beneath must be made visible, and in this case some oppositional design must certainly be used. In general, the natural inclination of the body to respond to emotion with movement has been largely suppressed by the discipline of good manners; physical reactions beyond the barest minimum are considered vulgar and uneducated. Well-brought-up people are trained never to flinch at bad news or pain, nor to clap each other on the back with joy. All etiquette will permit them is "mannerly" movement and a few discreetly chosen words, with a minimum of exaggeration. So the student must hunt in the highways and byways of behavior for the appropriate basic material. Some of this is to be found in residual traces of what people do, especially among the more "vulgar" and less suppressed, and from observing his own impulses, and from members of the acting profession, who make it their business to know what natural reactions are. A specific inquiry into the vocabulary of gesture and how it may be adapted to the dance follows later in the book. For the time being we merely try to find the design which will externalize the attitude to an idea. I add one more example of how this problem should be approached. Suppose the theme is "parting." In real life this action might reveal hardly a trace of the actual feeling. A person might be crushed, elated or angry, but pride or good manners will send him away walking much as he usually does. If the mood is "crushed," the dancer must find a design to express this. It will probably be successional in line—that is, having no oppositional energy—and asymmetrical, indicating a mood which has lost its balance.

Assignment

Compose designs which will show the attitude to a given idea, for one body, in space only. No movement is to be used beyond transitions.

When each student has three or four of these design positions, he is then asked to use the same ideas for two bodies instead of one. A preliminary explanation points out that the solo instrument can be quite elaborate, since it has the full responsibility of conveying the composer's meaning,

Think
IN THE MORNING

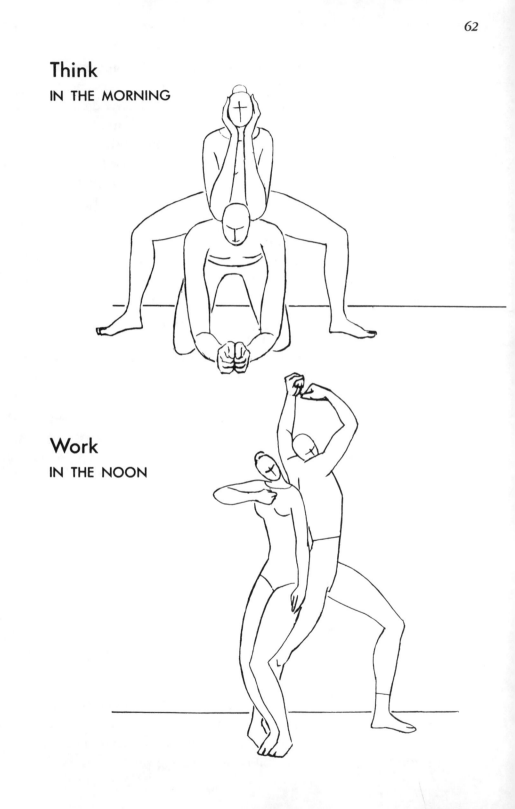

Work
IN THE NOON

Eat
IN THE EVENING

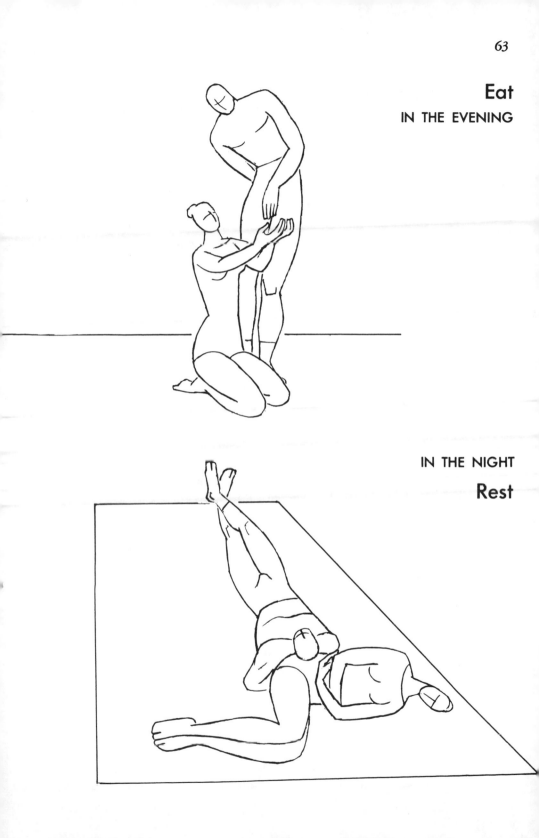

IN THE NIGHT
Rest

but as soon as even one other instrument is added, both must be simplified so as to complement each other; neither one is complete, and only together do they make a whole. A very clear illustration of this is the difference between a piano sonata and a trio of piano, violin and cello. In the sonata, the piano has the full development of the complete piece, but in the trio, it has only one voice, even though it may be the major one. In the music school this principle is understood as a matter of course, but dance composers often make the mistake of crowding more movement into a group than the eye can possibly grasp. The result is not a whole, but a number of wholes done at the same time. This is rather like all the instruments of an orchestra playing solo parts forte, which would give the listener a bad case of aural indigestion.

Even in the simple problem at hand—that of relating one figure to another in static design—the constant temptation is to overdo; I hear myself saying, "Too much," "Too many lines," "Eliminate half of it," over and over. Imagine how much more complex than this is the finished dance, all in movement, with costumes, music, lights, décor. If the basic clarity of design relationships is not there, the whole thing can easily be a jumble and a blur. The student is advised to make one of the two figures dominant and the other complementary, except of course in symmetrical design, which should always be used sparingly. The two bodies together should present a clear over-all design, either a succession or an opposition in symmetry or asymmetry. To be sure, there are many other ways of combining shapes, but these studies are deliberately simplified, like finger exercises. It has been my experience that the absolutely unerring eye for such design relationships is rare, but that this sense can be acquired very fast indeed; sometimes, by the end of one lesson all mistakes have been corrected with ingenuity and taste. Those with a well-developed visual sense will learn more quickly than those who grasp movement with the feelings and the muscles, but still the unmistakable signs of improvement in all students prove that design ideas can be taught.

There are two common errors to warn against in these duet design studies. One is the too-flat use of the bodies. If they are both in two-dimensional design, the effect will be remote, impersonal, like ritual figures. If the dancers are placed at contrasting angles to each other, or if the individuals are allowed to be three-dimensional to the eye, the full impact of the body is made use of. Two-dimensional design has its uses, but I prefer to stress the complete body to begin with. One other thing to look out for—the adventure of "making up" designs of this sort is likely to be very fascinating indeed, and can easily fall into a game, with the students trying to see how original they can be. "Too contrived" is a remark I make constantly, recalling to the student that flights of fancy too far removed from the original ideas, all of which are down to earth and familiar, are not expressive of them; and the very eccentric design calls too much attention to itself. Such a design would be very useful in comedy, satire or in a dance where "differentness" was the point, but it is not within the limits of the given problem.

This design exercise is meant to bring vividly to the eye the lesson that two bodies call for simpler lines than those for one body; also, the important point of contrast is again emphasized. It is well to remind the student that more bodies would necessitate more simplification, in the hope that he will remember this when it comes time to deal with a group. This does not mean that all solo figures should be very elaborate; they may or may not be, according to the theme. Nor does it mean that all group patterns must be starkly simple. It merely means that solos can be elaborately designed, but that ensembles cannot be very complex and retain their clarity or focus.

Since this assignment and the preceding one are static, the student is reminded that all this is not dancing, but an inquiry into the bones of design, with about as much relationship to movement as the study of a skeleton has to the whole body.

Assignment

Bring designs for two bodies on given ideas, no movement beyond transitions. This concludes, for the time being, an examination of the elements of design in space.

Design, Part 3

THE PHRASE

8 The other kind of design, that in time, now occupies our attention. This means that one space design will follow another, and that there will be a shape in their successions in time. Whether that shape will be like bits of mosaic put together at random, or whether it will present a time-picture to the mind which will be both logical and rememberable, is often the difference between improvisation and composition. Some people have a reliable instinct for the time-shape of movement and need no instruction in it. For the others, then, who need help in learning how to order movement in time, I offer the theory of the phrase, the name I use for the organization of movement in time-design.

The general shape of the phrase is something we have inherited from our most remote ancestors, going very far back into evolution. I identify this originally with the instinctive sounds issuing from millions of human throats in the course of expressing emotions of various kinds: fear, anger, contentment, mating urges, pain and others. These sounds, it seems to me, were developed over the long, laborious ages into a more conscious communication which resulted in language, and finally into the arts of literature and music. Even in the very earliest stages there was a time-shape in the sounds, which had two characteristics: their length was limited by the breath, and they had a rising and falling intensity and speed, due to their emotional basis. These instinctual utterances, I think, were phrases, and the ingredients of them are the same today as they were in the aboriginal era; that is, the modern communicative time-shape, in music, dance, or language, is in the length of a comfortable breath, and has rises and falls of feeling. We speak and sing, write melodic music, poetry and drama in phrases. Now movement, though not tied to the length of the breath—for one can very well dance without pausing for breath—is still very much influenced by the powerful emotional shape of the breath phrase, so that it, too, is more agreeable and comprehensible when phrased. Originally the movement and the sound were no doubt closely co-ordinated and followed similar patterns. Movement, dominated by the breath phrase, did not operate separately, but was commanded by the beginnings, endings and intensities which the sound itself motivated emotionally. For a vivid example of the subhuman origin of the phrase in both movement and sound, consider the cat fight—the ranges of pitch from pianissimo to forte, the climaxes, the growls, the spits, the yowls, all begun and ended on a breath! This is accompanied by lashes of the tail during the crescendo, slow stalks during the diminuendo, and then that fearful rush prestissimo with everything blazing at once. What a climax and what phrasing!

There is another, more pervasive and perhaps more compelling reason for the agreeableness of phrased movement, which we may define at this point as expenditure of energy at various rates, followed by a rest. The functions of the human body are "phrased" this way: The heart beats and rests; the lungs fill and subside; muscles demand rests from effort, as sustained tension results very quickly in exhaustion. There are other, longer phrases, like the energy-filled day, followed by the restful night; or the project that takes months of effort, followed by a vacation. Outside of the body, in the general world of matter, tension and relaxation also seem to operate as a law, at various rates of speed, so that this punctuation of energy is quite inescapable as a pattern. When the phrase-shape in this sense is disregarded, as it can be by artificial means in the arts, we are disconnected from this most fundamental of all shapes. Confronted with the loss, we feel anything from disinterestedness and boredom to downright exhaustion. The author who writes page-long sentences has us breathless and tired; hot jazz played for a whole evening without a break is intolerable except to the most insensitive; long stretches of dancing which are unphrased are particularly exhausting because of the kinesthetic association of our bodies with the dancer. Conversely, the very short statement is thoroughly unsatisfactory, too. Here the rests are so frequent that the breathing rate is much too short and therefore irritating. Children write thusly: "My cat is black. My house is white. My cat likes milk. My mommy likes me." Sophisticated dancing and writing are often like this, too; short, stabbing and stimulating, up to the point where we "can't catch our breath."

It is a lamentable fact that many dances are composed and performed with a total unawareness of phrasing. There are discernible reasons for this: In dancing it is easy to "keep going"; the trained body can get its needed muscle rest very quickly by changing from one part to another and by minute and imperceptible stops between movements. Dancers are often afraid to stop moving for fear of not being exciting. Actually the opposite is true; if they don't stop, they certainly will be boring. Many a time I have used the reverse of the old admonition and said, "Don't just do something, stand there!"

There is a great deal of evidence that, although dance as an art has no compelling physical reason for phrasing itself—as, for instance, singing has —still the onlooker enjoys it much more if it is shaped according to the familiar pattern of effort and rest. There is another point of information, coming from outside the dance world, which supports this. Scientists have long noted the fact that the human mind has a proclivity for grouping experience in patterns; people are happier when a maze of sensation can be sorted out into some kind of order. The viewer of dance instinctively wants to understand the order of it, and the phrase-pattern is one thing which he can perceive. Without this, it quite easily becomes a labyrinth of movement, distracting and puzzling. He wants to catch his own breath comfortably as the performance is going on.

Obviously the dance that is not intended to be a communicative art is not, and need not be, concerned with the phrase. The religious ceremonial which goes on from dark to dawn in primitive tribes has quite another objective. Its purpose is to insure the benignity of the gods by magical means, and this calls for much repetition of the sacred formula, which may be like one long drone. Sophisticated outsiders, even those who love the picturesque, can seldom endure the monotony of one of these ceremonials for twenty-four hours at a time. It is not a show. Similarly, all recreational dancing is for doing, not seeing. Folk art, to be acceptable in the theater, has to undergo some judicious staging, not the least of which is canny phrasing by some knowing director.

The good dance, then, should be put together with phrases, and the phrase has to have a recognizable shape, with a beginning and an end, rises and falls in its over-all line, and differences in length for variety. The phrase should never be in a monotone, for the reason, stated previously, that dance is in the realm of feeling, which is never in a straight horizontal line. There are endless varieties of the phrase, but for practical purposes they may be divided into three simple categories: the high point at the beginning; the high point at or near the end; the high point at or near the middle. By high point, I do not necessarily mean high

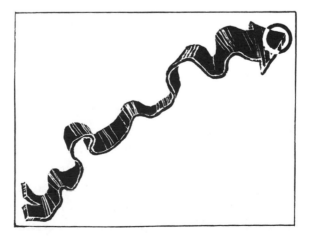

in space; it might be achieved by a stronger dynamic, an increase in tempo, or some other element of movement. (See diagrams on page 69 of dance phrases indicating climax at beginning middle or end.)

To begin to compose a phrase, the student is asked to recall the material of his first assignment, the nine "words," one of which he will now attempt to make into a sentence, or phrase. The analogy to language cannot be followed exactly in this process. All the words are not to be strung together into a sentence, for they are in a sense like nouns which need the other parts of language to support and round them out. For the dancer, there are several devices which can be used to accomplish this, which are so different from the organization of language that words do not serve very well to describe them.

First, the intent of the one-bar material should be recalled, and one of the three shapes of the phrase decided on as most suitable to it. Suppose the original idea was an eager advance followed by a slight hesitation of uncertainty. The student may wish to base most of the phrase on the uncertainties, and conclude with the positive idea. The high point would therefore be at the end. Or he might start with a great burst of courage which diminishes to a faltering end. Another interpretation might call for a climax in the middle. In any case he has some material for "eagerness advancing," and some for "hesitation," which must be developed to give it a phrase length. If the student thinks he can do this improvisationally, he should be encouraged to try, but usually he needs some help with the manipulation of material. One of the devices is fragmentation. Instead of stating the whole movement which he has for "hesitation," he may break it up into small parts, which may be added one to the other, so as to be accumulated into the whole. Connecting material may be put between them— as, for instance, walking or running steps—so that much more space is covered and more time used than in the original. Alterations in vertical space may be introduced. If the original movements are in the medium plane, they may be heightened by jumping or lowering the body to the floor. Changes in direction are permissible, too; and variations in rhythm, tempo and dynamics. In spite of the fact that many of these factors have yet to be explored thoroughly, it is necessary to introduce them here in order to construct the phrase with any comprehensiveness. This elongation of the "word" is not fitted into a count. Rather, it is put together with dramatic timing, and the length of it is, as nearly as one can put it, a breath. These breaths, of course can and should vary in duration, as they are not literally the length of one breath of the body at rest, but rather like a spoken sentence, with possibly a subclause or two; or, using another comparison, like the melodic line a flutist might play in one breath. The student may often err in judgment as to the right length of one of these phrases when he is performing his own work, but the eyes of those who watch have a positively uncanny accuracy in this matter. There is usually a hundred per cent agreement as to whether it is too long or too short, and students can safely be trusted to tell each other.

Probably the most important factor in the successful composition of one of these phrases is the quality of the original material in the "word." As in the making of any other product, first-class ingredients are essential for superior results. Poor craftsmanship can ruin them, of course. One should have both skill and substance to work with. The ability to build well (a good sense of form) without the imagination to invent good materials (movement) does exist, especially among those who have not been weaned away from a set vocabulary, but usually the inventive mind seizes on all parts of the problem equally well.

There are other ways of constructing a phrase—rhythmically instead of dramatically, for instance—but since the analysis of rhythm is yet to come, I prefer starting with feeling, which is simpler and was the original motivation for the nine "words."

Assignment

Make a phrase from one of the nine "words" of the first assignment in a breath length, using dramatic timing, for one body.

Design, Part 4

THE STAGE SPACE

9 The moment the student is permitted to move in space (in the phrase assignment) with free choice as to his direction and position, it is at once apparent that he needs some basis for using space other than his untrammeled and unreliable instinct. Since he is engaged in learning the techniques of a stage art, he must now be made aware of the special significance of this particular space, which has attributes and dimensions and purposes quite different from any other space. In particular, it differs radically from the physical and psychological space of the studio, where he has learned about his body for so many years, and where he is even now acquiring knowledge about choreography. If it were practical, all composition classes should be held on a stage. Then the laborious explanation which follows would be partly unnecessary, and certainly more comprehensible. For a stage is a highly specialized kind of space—not, like a studio, bounded by four walls, windows, mirrors, chairs, and whatnot; nor is it wide open like a meadow or a beach; nor is it, for the most part, in the round, as are some modern stages for plays. Dancers are still likely to function for a long time on the traditional picture-frame stage. The student should be led away from his understandable feeling that dancing is movement of the body and can be placed just anywhere that is convenient in the space at his command. This introspective concentration on the movement has been instilled in him by years of class work, in which the only space consideration was to find room enough to work without interfering with other people. In this respect the dance student is at a disadvantage in comparison to the drama student, who has some technical training without space considerations (sitting in chairs for voice training and reading), but very early in the proceedings is put into a "scene." He, however awkwardly, has to make entrances and exits, keep a convincing relationship to other people, learn to sit down, walk around at proper moments and in the right places. In short, he is very early learning the business of the actor in his workshop and final showshop—the stage.

Compared to this, dance training, with its years and years of technique in a studio, is very incomplete and unrealistic indeed. Sometimes the student never learns anything about the stage. He is merely transferred from the studio to a company rehearsing on a stage, for a performance where he is directed in every move he makes; and probably the total advice about stage space is contained in the words of the director: ". . . and don't knock into the legs on the exit." (What legs? My legs? Her legs?) Dancers of my generation were mostly brought up in the theater, and such appalling ignorance was unknown, but now it is commonplace. It seems obvious, with even the most superficial thought on the subject, that the stage, a place for communication, has some very special attributes spatially, which can be made to help choreography or injure it, according to the understanding of the composer. To begin to make the stage come alive as a special place, I try as far as possible to transform the studio into a stage, by marking areas with chairs, by word description, and finally by moving a dancer in this imaginary space to illustrate the various points. Since we are free to build our space ideally in the studio, we choose proportions which give the body the freedom which it needs, and yet frame it snugly. For the single dancer of medium proportions, a space about 28 by 20 feet is comfortable—not so immense that the body seems swallowed up, nor so small that big movement must be cramped. For groups, this stage should be enlarged to 35 by 28 feet, more or less, according to the number of dancers involved. Probably never again will the choreographer have just the stage dimensions he needs. Theater designers, being an erratic lot, and bound by all sorts of considerations of economy and imperious boards of directors as well, come up with creations ranging from handkerchief-size stages, with no wings, to something 90 feet wide and 20 feet deep, or dome-shaped eccentricities with one exit. (Also, of course, a few very good ones indeed.)

In the studio, the oblong stage is marked at its four corners; for the single dancer, the proscenium arch is imagined, the sides and back are filled in with make-believe curtains and legs, and we are ready to talk about the magical place where dreams will come alive.

First, let us remember what visions have inhabited this extraordinary boxlike space. It seems to me that a few reminders of the great who have trod the boards and the magnificent plays which have uplifted the heart are in order, and I quote Ruth St. Denis, who said, "I never in my life set my feet on a stage without thinking of its magic and my destiny." I would like to emphasize this space so that never in their lives will students walk on it heedlessly, as though it were a humdrum thing like a baseball diamond or the lobby of a hotel. If the talk of hallowed ground grows semi-mystical, this seems not too much for young people, who are apt to think, "A floor is a floor, and it's to hold me up while I am dancing, isn't it?" I say, "That place just behind the entrance, before you take the first step out, is just a board, a private place for you to gather your forces, merely a wooden support for your flight into magic. It is your own, to do with as you wish, and of no concern to anyone else. But the moment you emerge, you belong to the theater, a public place, where fate has miraculously allowed you to make your tiny contribution to the art. If you can utter one word as potent as any of Shakespeare's, or as moving as Modjeska's, how privileged you should feel!"

If I could design a studio or a training theater, I would have the off-stage spaces painted a practical, nonexciting color—say, brown—and the whole stage in pools of color, to emphasize first its luminosity, and second, its extreme differences in area. This space would only be for dancing, never for technique classes. Failing this, we must try to imagine these things.

First, consider the four corners. These are architecturally supported by powerful verticals. Those in the back, made by a leg and the edge of the backdrop, will symmetrically frame an emerging figure; down front, the proscenium vertical and the leg directly behind it have a great effect on the figure. Stand a dancer in any of the four corners and note what happens. The upper two make the figure seem important with a remoteness which suggests, if there is no other specific mood, a heroic beginning. The powerful verticals energize the body; it seems to be upheld by walls of both physical and spiritual strength. To sense this more completely, imagine the same figure standing at one side of a field of clover with an immense sky above; the figure might be the focus of the scene, but would be weakened rather than strengthened by the environment. The two upper corners, far more than the downstage two, convey a strong impression of significant beginnings because they have not only the two verticals, but lines racing to them from various parts of the stage to form right angles—always makers of conflict and power. There are two of these from the top and two at the stage level, which, with the two verticals, make six strong supports in the upper two corners. Add to these one more factor: the invisible diagonals which stream from the upper corners to the lower. These are certainly there, in spite of the fact that you cannot see them. Put the dancer to walking on one of these diagonals from up right to down left, and he is moving on the most powerful path on the stage. Even without his lifting a finger, the eye will clothe this figure with a heroic strength, all made merely by the use of the architecture of stage space. (See diagram below, indicating invisible diagonals.)

Note some changes in emphasis as this figure walks slowly on its diagonal way. Two steps away from the corner, the six supporting lines no longer operate, and the figure is alone on an adventure in which he leaves his stronghold. He even seems too courageous and foolish in leaving his fortified corner, yet we are aware that he must fare forth and test his own strength. There is a precarious weak spot on the way—the corner is far behind, the fortress of the center not yet gained. Will this expose his weakness or will he resolutely carry himself on, with the original momentum and purpose? Now the power of the center begins to fortify him—the center, where there is no precarious conflict, which

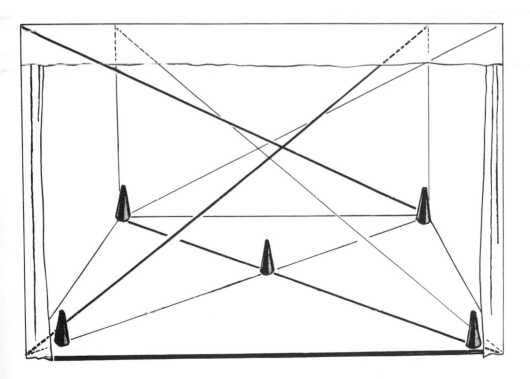

balances him and upholds him. I have often tried to estimate the number of forces operating on the center of a stage and never quite decided on the whole array. I should say there are at least eleven lines converging on it, plus the psychological security of the symmetrical design. This, commonly called by its misnomer, "dead center," is without doubt the most powerful single spot on the stage, yet there is a curious weakness about it, too. After being made aware of the strength of the center, students will compose whole sections, even complete dances, in this area. But after a short while, the power begins to fade, almost as though the electricity had failed. Very soon, unless the movement is completely absorbing, we are restless; the magic of the center is gone. In fact, all the areas seem to have a sensitive waxing and waning rhythm. Any of them will wear out with overuse and must be refreshed and energized by rest. No rules can be laid down for anything so intangible as this. It's a question of learning by advice and experience.

Our dancer has now gained the center, and he is at his fullest strength (all without any movement except walking) We rejoice for him, but he does not stop or linger. The glory of the climax begins to fade.

We see him moving toward the downstage corner and oblivion. We know he must traverse another dangerous place, the weak spot between the center and the corner, but we do not fear the menace of it because the end is so near. He reaches the proscenium. Its vertical is reminiscent of the original departure. Is it perhaps another home, not so strong but familiar, or is it the entrance to a tomb? The figure vanishes, cut off like a knife thrust by the final engulfing vertical. Just a simple walk, but how dramatic and pulsating in all its implications! One other thing: On his journey, as he comes near to the downstage exit, this human being changes from someone impersonal, remote, whom we do not know, to a friend, someone we care about. As he reaches the exit, where he is close to us, we are concerned about him. He is no longer an abstraction but a fellow human being.

Now consider the downstage corners. They are by no means so powerful; converging lines are fewer, and the main characteristic is the personal element. We cannot believe in the power or symbolic meaning of one entering here; he is one of us, dressed up; he is too revealed in all detail of personality and appearance. Moreover, he cannot move on that Via Triumphalis given to the upstage figure. He can, of course, walk on

the diagonal from downstage to up, but will become weaker as he goes because his back is to us, and also because he is retreating, not advancing. He could walk backwards and so give us his face, but this would do very little good, and even verge on the comical. There are other directions in which he could move after entering—straight across, for instance—but this would continue to make him personal. You cannot say anything serious or important on the footlights unless it is a speech at a bond rally. This is the place for comedy—and personality pitches. Comedians nearly fall over the edge in their reliable instinct to be closer, and they are quite right, too. People who enter in downstage corners can only become more personal, as they move on stage, or more remote and recessive. (See page 77 for example of entrance from downstage corner.)

Sometimes the downstage corners are good for exits, however. These can move us very much if they are preceded by sequences which are placed in powerful areas, and which call for the flippant, the personal or the dashing conclusion. Exits downstage can even be ominous or tragic, if the idea calls for culmination in personal torment. For instance, at the end of José Limón's "Exiles," Adam and Eve slowly exit downstage as they leave Paradise to enter their world of sorrow and suffering. We are made to identify with them in a personal way, as our first ancestors. An upstage exit for these two would have made the whole thing seem mythical; we would not have had a sense of immediacy. The whole lesson to be learned here is that stage areas will support and enhance various conceptions, or they will negate them, and it is necessary for the choreographer to make conscious choices.

One could stay with just the four corners and their diagonals for a long time. Many fascinating experiments will occur to the student and the teacher. For example, deliberately try to build a diagonal sequence from an up corner to downstage, which will stress strong climactic movement in the two weak areas and be timid in the three strong places. This might start either on stage or with an entrance in a corner, using vague, indecisive movement; rise to a sharp, strong accent between the corner and the center; be irresolute and weak in the center itself; and so forth to the ending, which might have a collapse below the vertical proscenium. This would seem to be the expression of a perverse and neurotic personality. If that is the goal, then this is one of the ways to do it. Then repeat the same movements, using the normal matching of strong and weak movements with the corresponding areas. Immediately the figure is restored to health and sanity, with only enough undynamic passages to indicate rest, and the gathering of force toward another effort. Another experiment: Try a short collapsing sequence in different areas of the diagonal. In the up corner this will seem remote, sick, impersonal, like an animal in hiding. In the next place, the weak one between that and the center, the matching weaknesses will make us feel—yes, this is an area for despair, but the desparation is far away, pathetic, lonely; we cannot care much. In the center, the denial of life seems tragic, even heroic. The following weak area engages our sympathy, especially because it is so near a psychological haven of safety, the downstage vertical, and the collapse at the corner could be quite unbearable, the cease of energy just as the goal is reached. A similar sequence could be tried with the opposite mood, all aggression and vitality. Then very interesting deductions can be drawn about comedy from an attempt to be amusing in these various places. It would be a real feat to be funny in an upstage corner. Everything conspires against it. It is too remote, too mythical a place, and even Danny Kaye would find this difficult. (You'll always find Danny and the rest of them right in the laps of their audience.) The only places where comedy might be successful at all would be in the second half, from the center to downstage. Distance is the enemy of humor, and severe architectural shape is, too. The psychology of the absurd must reduce the human being to ordinary proportions or he takes on a very unfunny seriousness. Naturally, there are exceptions. A satire on pomposity, for instance, might take advantage of the grandeur of the formidable corners, and be devastatingly stuffed-shirtish in the center. But for the light touch in general, no part of this diagonal is really good. It should be played much farther downstage. To explain these things seems very obvious indeed, yet I have seen students try to be amusing against the back wall, where we couldn't care less, hug the center too long, and make all the other mistakes possible. To draw a not-very-precise comparison, the stage is like a piano keyboard; the finger must touch exactly the right note or all is lost.

One other manipulation of corner-diagonal space is most revealing, and even astonishing. Call for piano accompaniment for some of these sequences. The ear will tell us much about the mood and the character of the performance. A straightforward accompaniment following the strong-weak movement alternations will be normal, though perhaps unexciting, because of lack of contrast. If it fits the accents and movements exactly, it will really be boring. Now reverse this procedure. If soft sound supports strong movement and vice versa, a curious effect is produced. The music seems to be antagonist; the figure of the dancer fights to be strong without encouragement; and in his more vulnerable moods the music seems to seek to destroy and dominate him. But the dancer will be the stronger of the two; the eye supersedes the ear. It is like a dialogue. Music can also completely distort the mood. Suppose the dancer has a sequence arranged which is quite serious, a small segment of one of life's major encounters. Accompany this by trivial music which patters along without any depth of feeling. The result is that the dancer does not become stronger by contrast; rather he seems empty, silly and pretentious. Such is the power of the sound to set the mood. This same sequence, accompanied by jaunty, slightly jazzy music, can make the dancer look cynical; he is pretending to be serious, but actually it is all bluff, and he believes in nothing. The variations on this kind of thing are endless. I am afraid that, for the most part, neither choreographers nor composers are aware of these mutations and subleties of combination. They almost always just play it straight, and together.

Other areas of the stage, and their significance, I will mention briefly. The whole of the center is extremely potent, from the farthest point back to the edge in front. But "dead center" is the exact high point of this. Have a figure walk slowly down center from back to front. When farthest away he is mysterious, with a high dynamic and symbolic potential, much more so than if he were off center. As he advances, the electrically charged center takes over and he increases in stature and in power. Now note that as he moves to the apron, although he looms larger physically, the power diminishes rapidly, and on the footlights—or where the footlights used to be—we see this is a fellow student with a name, blonde hair, and such and such a figure; in short, a real, nonmagical and nonpotent young lady, not conveying, or able to convey, any meaning beyond the folksy and the commonplace. This is not the fault of the young lady, but of the place where she stands. Should she attempt to be tragic or heroic at this spot, she would be embarrassing, even to the point of satire. Al Jolson sang "Mammy" right on the edge of the stage, and his popularity soared, but Cleopatra must never come down to the footlights. To use a cliche, distance lends enchantment, which is never so true as in dancing. (See page 81 for significance of center.)

In commenting on the relative values of directions in movement, I say that straight forward is most powerful because the body and the whole dynamic of the dancer make a direct communication; diagonal is next, then side to side, and then around. Around movement, whether in a turn by a single dancer, or in a circular pattern by a group, can be exciting if done with virtuoso technique, but the angles of the bodies change so rapidly that line communication and design are almost obliterated, leaving only a physical feat as the stimulating element. The sight of a group composed of many bodies moving rapidly in a circle is rousing chiefly by the sheer repetition of physical vitality. The circle doesn't say anything, unless it is that life is endless; it only moves, and carries us around with it. This is not to disparage the circle. The sense of continuity it gives is often just the right keynote for the theme. As an example of the weakening effect

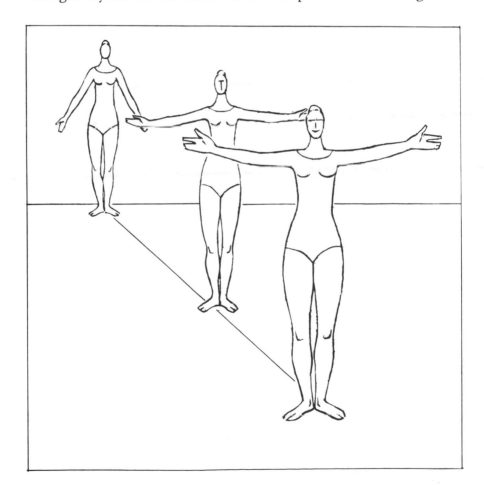

of the circle, imagine a dancer who wants to establish a characterization of some imperious historical queen. It would be quite wrong to plan it so that the lady entered in the middle of the side (a very weak place to begin or end anything) and began moving in a circular pattern. No matter how dramatic or ingenious the movement, the changing angles and the softness of the circle will be bound to weaken the idea. How much better to establish this figure mostly facing forward, with a few, possibly very simple gestures, so that we immediately know this person and are aware of her inner mood through direct communication.

As a simple rule of thumb, there are six weak areas and seven strong ones on a stage (see diagram below). Also add the fact that movement, though personal on the footlights and therefore only suitable for intimate moods, loses power as it retreats upstage—except at dead center. Remember that the main paths which are illuminated, so to speak, are the diagonals and down the center; that the sides are very weak for either entrances or exits, or any movement. In fact, all places except the corners and center back are weak for emergences or departures. Innumerable studies can be devised to sample the flavor of these areas. Left far behind is the idea that a stage floor is just another kind of support, and it becomes more like a sensitive musical instrument to play on. I urge students not to think of it as static, but dynamic, full of vibration and sound, with the composer in control of the volume.

I have been commenting on the natural meanings of stage space, which are, by the way, for the most part, unique in the dance. Drama has

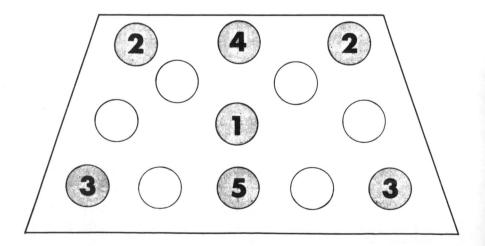

other uses for stages, partly because at no time will the space be as wide open as it is for the dance. The themes of plays, operas, etc., often demand a great deal of furniture or set. No actor has a chance to walk on that magical diagonal. In the first place, it is unlikely that there will be an entrance in the corner, and then on the way are a sofa, a cocktail table, several chairs and people. The space problems are entirely different. I must confess to a great enthusiasm for that bare open space, inhabited by nothing but dancers, which is given to movement composers. Also, I feel a pang of sympathy for the opera or spectacle choreographer, who has to make an impression with dancing under the most difficult circumstances. All too often, twenty or more dancers are crowded into a handkerchief-size space, not supported visually by anything but a large chorus in loud motley colors, several soloists placed well downstage to catch the eye, much elaborate scenery, steps, fountains, doorways, house façades, banners or whatnot—a first-class clutter to contend with. No wonder opera ballet is generally considered to be quite far down on the artistic scale.

Although the stage can be treated for dancing by using just its natural powers, and should be so studied, various techniques can very well alter the plain open stage. Lighting is one of these elements. If there is, for instance, a very good reason for not being able to use a strong area for a strong idea, the lighting can come to the rescue. Lighting will build the climaxes, obliterate figures when it is desirable not to see them, and in innumerable ways play a valuable part in the structure of the choreography. The man who controls the switchboard is an artist playing a sensitive instrument, with as much variety of timbre as an orchestra. It is not too extravagant to say that many a mediocre dance has been "dressed" by expert lighting to look like a near masterpiece. It behooves the choreographer to inform himself about lighting, and take it into account in the composing process as a valuable tool. In this day it is much too naïve to compose a dance in a studio and then merely dump it on a stage like a car in a salesroom. (Not a very good comparison—oh, those automobile shows with dramatic pink spots!)

Other alterations of the plain open space involve props or sets. These can either support the natural dynamics and architecture or place emphasis in unnatural places. This is quite legitimate as long as it makes some sense—that is, serves a functional or dramatic purpose. I hope we are beyond the era when bits of things are scattered around for decorative effect, or when backdrops, executed by easel painters, all but obliterate the dancers.

Since we are considering the proscenium stage and its potential, this seems an appropriate place to comment on projection, which causes problems very different from those of the dancer in the studio. On a conventional stage, there is one side only—the window, or opening—that can be used for communication. This calls for many adjustments of focus and even of movement if the full impact is to reach an audience. There are both psychological and physical aspects of projection. The dancer who moves with confidence will command our attention because he is projecting his assurance. The dancer with conviction has power; many a dance of poor quality has been "put across" just by the superb belief of the performer in the work. In other words, if you believe in yourself, everybody else probably will, too. Conversely, there have been many tragic first performances where excellently composed works have been all but ruined by the jitters of the performers. How does one acquire confidence? Ask the psychologists. But every director can help in establishing some measure of security, and there are various useful little tricks of deep breathing, relaxation, and so forth. For the deep-seated case of stage fright, there is really no known remedy, although a thousand successful performances can usually effect a cure if the performer can live through the first five hundred of them.

Physical projection involves many points to remember. The first is an awareness of the rising bank of people "out front," from below stage level to anywhere from twenty- to fifty-foot-high balconies, and, in some theaters, boxes on the side. The careful director will take note of the sight lines from the extreme side aisles and avoid setting every important movement so far out of line that a quarter of the house cannot see it. Fortunately, old theaters, particularly opera houses, where a third of the audience can only see half the stage, are being abandoned. Still, there are many of these left, and for those people who have to sit in inexpensive seats for performances, the only source of information as to what really happened is the review written by the critic who was sitting plunk in the middle of the orchestra.

When working on projection in a studio, I stress the fact that communication with the audience is the keynote, and explain that the whole focus of the movement must be lifted out and up. Students must abandon the conversational level which they grow used to in a studio, where the dancers, the teacher and any visitors are all on the same horizontal line. To project effectively to the balconies, heads and eyes must be higher, and a conscious sense of distance must be developed. Many a time the student is too absorbed in the complications of his work to remember this, and it takes constant reminders to retrain him. "You're not talking to the man in the balcony" is something they hear *ad nauseam.* Old movies in the grand manner are illuminating and delightful in this respect. I remember a picture of Sarah Bernhardt in "La Dame aux Camélias." She was standing in a doorway upstage. Frequently during the emotional speech there was a lift of her beautiful head, and her eyes communicated to the last row of the gallery. This was artificial, yes, but justifiably so, for purposes of projection. Acting these days is usually so natural that balcony audiences see only the tops of heads, and hear a vague mumble. Dancing, being much more stylized than acting anyway, not only should, but must, employ the art of projection, however unnatural this may seem to the realists. In this respect there are important adjustments of body lines to be kept in mind, too. The full impact of the body should be directed to the front whenever possible. This does not mean that dancers should stare into the balcony and always face front, but it does mean that many adjustments should be made as to the face and body directions.

I am not a believer in the faceless dancer. I cannot go along with the cult which holds that a face is just something to carry around on the neck, and that all meaning is in the body. In everyday communication, we talk to faces, read faces, respond primarily to expressions and words coming from faces. Imagine how disconcerting it would be if all our friends decided that it was highly improper to move their eyes and the muscles of their faces; gave up smiles, nods, frowns; and we were asked to talk to them as if they were stones. I see no reason for eliminating expression of the face, either in private conversation or on the stage, and the absence of animation seems highly arbitrary and irrational to me. I am assuming, of course, that the aim is human communication. If the purpose is otherwise—for example, impersonality and total abstraction—then the impassive face is appropriate.

The lines of the body can be all but obliterated by improper choices of direction, and a great deal of effort can be wasted when the movement does not clearly address itself to the one open side of the stage. For instance, a dancer, facing off stage and standing in second position, with his arms to the side, is throwing away about half his body. Just as it is absolutely elementary for the actor to be heard, so the dancer must be seen. I know it is most disconcerting for a young composer who has put a great deal of heart and thought into a study or a dance to be told, "This is at the wrong angle and makes the arms invisible. Don't leave me with your back and no face for so long; arrange a different leap; I cannot see the legs." Sometimes the "dont's" become so frustrating that it is better to ignore some of the minor mistakes for the sake of giving the student a sense of accomplishment. (See below for right and wrong examples.)

The classic ballet solved the problem of projection by the simplest means. The choreographer very well knew that forward, forward diagonal and circular movement would insure plenty of projection and face. So, after the execution of a step in one of these directions, which carried the dancer downstage, he was merely directed to walk around to an upstage

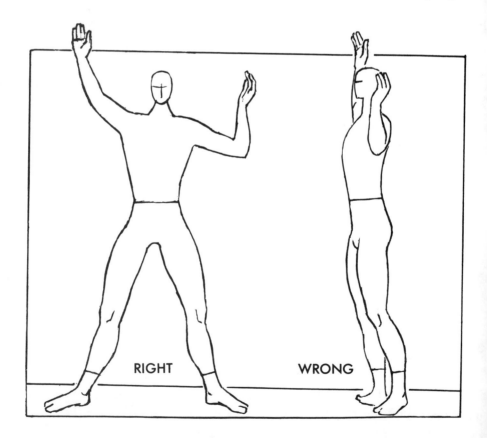

position, until he could again be in a place to move forward. I suspect this also gave the dancer a much-needed rest. Anyway, the elegant "walk-around" is still one of the characteristics of a classic dance, although choreographers now consider it a point of honor to be able to devise movement which will be ingenious enough to avoid this old-fashioned device.

There is another aspect of projection which should not be neglected while we are dealing with stage space. This is the bow. The bow is the end after the ending and is extremely important as the final statement of the dancer. I believe bows should be composed carefully, even if they are to look spontaneous and natural. Of all the elements in a bow, space awareness is the most important. The essence of it is "thank you" from a host to presumably delighted guests. First of all we have to find the guests, who are en masse, but scattered, and are congratulating the party-giver *tutti*. In the old days, the elite sat in the orchestra and in boxes; the royal family was in a special box, sometimes near the stage, sometimes center; and the hoi polloi sat in the gallery. The niceties of etiquette demanded acknowledgement first to any members of the blood royal, then the aristocracy and finally, but not least, the common people, who were not so blasé as to talk and flirt through the all-giving of the artist, and were cherished for it. This classified audience made the bows an easy matter: first the royal box, then the boxes to each side (one after the other), then the orchestra and lastly the gallery. They were done separately, with a little pause beween each, and with the dancer always being careful to change the feet, and face the whole body in the proper direction. This extreme formality scarcely exists any more. In its place there is often a deplorable bobbing and scuttling which lacks both graciousness and dignity. It seems to me that on a nongala occasion, where there are no flag-draped boxes and no particular protocol to observe, the formal bow should be patterned something after the following: An advance to center downstage, the first bow to begin high at the balcony level and carry down to the orchestra in one continuous movement. If this is to be elaborated, two more bows are added, from one side to the other. If there is only a single dancer, the triple bow will not be too much. If there are many solo-ists, the single up-and-down bow will be plenty, or proceedings will go on to a ridiculous length. One other thing: The general direction of the bow is forward, but includes a retreat, so that, after the single bow is done down-

RIGHT   WRONG

RIGHT   WRONG

stage, it is followed by a few steps backward and a repeat upstage. Very much like a host backing away from his guests with a series of farewells as he goes toward his own front door.

The bow is really a fascinating problem, full of pitfalls as to timing, manner, projection and style. Bows should differ according to the dance they follow. Those for comedy can be faster, even border on the cute, but those which are for serious or tragic dances should be in a rhythm and manner to maintain the mood. What a shock to see a tragedy queen who has moved you by her performance come out with a smile which shows how pleased she is with herself, but destroys your enjoyment of the dance! Bows are also extremely revealing of personality. The condescending or arrogant bow of a young dancer who you thought was a sweet lovely child reveals depths and forebodings for the future which are very disturbing. Equally upsetting is the duck-and-run bow which follows a dance full of poise and dignity.

Students must be trained in these procedures and encouraged to think about and work on the proper bow, not leaving this important affair to a last-minute dress rehearsal. I have even known bows not to be rehearsed at all. A solo dancer can usually handle himself reasonably well, but groups must really be drilled. When you see a good ensemble bow, you can rest assured it has had some painstaking work put in on it, as there are endless difficulties to overcome. Dancers lag, they forget to come in, forget to go out, talk in the wings, can't remember the timing or the number of curtains, and they bow to the worms. With a sense of humor one can rather enjoy this as a comedy of errors. Nothing is so hilarious as the one small dancer who is still bowing when everyone else has made an exit. Or the panic on the faces of those who have come in at the wrong time. Instinctively they all want to bow to Lilliputian people about two feet from the ends of their toes. The one direction which must be repeated most is, "Move the focus higher." In brief, the spatial and social meaning of the bow has to be trained into dancers like any other technique.

Since stages in the round are now so much in vogue, some consideration of these in regard to choreography is certainly in order. (Television, motion picture and special stages of this kind involve so many different procedures that I shall make no attempt to discuss them.) Circular stages abound, especially in little theaters and summer music tents—and dance is invited in. To begin bluntly, my opinion is that these circular stages are highly injurious to the dance. This is for a very obvious reason. The dance is a visual art, but, unlike good sculpture, it is not equally arresting from all angles; it is at its best from only one direction. In this it is completely different from the aural arts. The soprano with her back to you is perhaps not quite as good as she would be straight on, but still the tone is there and most of the art is intact. This is also true of dialogue in a play. The word is the thing. As long as you can hear it, you have the gist of the play, although you may miss a little of the "business" if you are back of the players. The advocates of the theater in the round stress intimacy. So many more people can be close to the actors, and thus the impact is intensified, they say. This can be valid for a play, especially for situations which are about ordinary people, with whom we can indentify easily. I can imagine "Our Town" or "The Glass Menagerie" gaining by the participation of an audience which is almost on the stage with the actors.

But there is a vast difference between a play and a dance. Any dance, even the most folksy, is much more stylized than a play. What, to the dancers, is an ordinary walking step is already so distorted—or, if you prefer, idealized—that no character in a play would ever walk that way. This means to me that more intimacy does not help the dancer, because he does not seek to be more real and natural but more stylized and magical. To be too close to the magician, so that you catch him in his tricks of manipulation, is to destroy all the fun of the illusion. For these reasons, it seems to me that the picture-frame stage, or the one-side projection only, is far preferable for the aims of the dance.

I can see a reason for a few exceptions, however. For example, the annual Hanukkah celebrations held in enormous arenas are spectacles for the thousands. Here folk dancing is in order, frequently in circles or geometric formations which are almost equally good from any side. As one element in a massive epic, dance of the folk variety, not depending on dramatic or linear projection, does not fare too badly. In fact, the spectacle must have it; where would the celebration be without the big dance?

Assignment

Bring in a study making use of stage space, plus a bow appropriate to it. Try to include elements from former studies, such as the phrase, a contrast in dynamics, design, rhythm and motivation.

Design, Part 5

SMALL GROUPS

10   "Group" is a word which, as applied to dance, came in with modern-dance companies. Ensembles, before that, were known as the corps de ballet, or just dancers, as distinguished from principals. There is an implicit social difference here, which made the word "group" emerge to define a new relationship between the participants in a dance form geared to a demo-cratic idea. Rank in the ballet world was and is still derived from the hierarchy of the court, beginning with the king and queen, then the nobles, the commoners, and lastly the lackeys and servants. Dancers progressed from their school days through exactly this sort of social strata, which only differed from the real thing in the fact that commoners could become kings. Once a young woman became a prima ballerina assoluta, she was assured of her queenly position until she could function no longer, and there was no question of her ever again mixing with the common people. But it is commonplace nowadays to find dancers serving as both soloists and ensemble performers at various times.

Not only does this democratic procedure alter the functioning of the dancers, but it changes the very shape of choreographic form as well. No longer, or rarely, does the ensemble warm up the proceedings with some-thing fairly innocuous, and then line up to receive royalty in the form of the prima ballerina and/or her partner. Ensemble dances in classic style used to have very little importance. They merely introduced the work, and in between kept the attention of audiences while the soloists prepared to dazzle again in the spotlight. But they were very useful for making a great hurra-burra at the end, with a bravura finale. A stage full of people all jumping and turning, with soloists in the middle, was the standard con-clusion of nineteenth-century ballet, and is often used even today.

Modern dance had an entirely different conception of relationships. Groups were not anonymous, nor were they the humblest and least talented dancers at the command of a director. Strenuous efforts were made to train and develop personality in a company because the role of the group had become vitally important. Sometimes the whole weight of the dance was on the shoulders of the group; individuals were comparatively unimportant, acting more as a focus and as a contrast than as kings and queens worshiped by their subjects. Many early modern dances could be cited as examples of this new attitude to people, and therefore to choreography. One of them was my composition "The Shakers," done about 1931, in which the ensemble was dominant. There was a center figure, yes, but by far the strongest and most important movement was given to the group, and it was their collective strength which gave power to the dance. It is obvious that such a profound change in social attitude would have a radical effect on choreography, and would free it from some very conventional forms which had grown stiff with age. In classic Greece and in Egypt, and other early civilizations, the chorus had an honored part in all plays and festivals. Some of the most memorable and eloquent passages in all dramatic literature were lovingly designed to be spoken by choric-dramatic ensembles on great occasions. All this passed away with the glory that was Greece, and not until the twentieth century did the chorus come back. It was the modern dance and, to some extent, the popular musical which restored it. Now it is not uncommon for the nominal star of a company to make an unobtrusive entrance, along with several other people, in a busy part of the stage. This, among other things, has a curious fascination about it. Audiences are alert and intrigued, wondering, "Where will he come in this time?", and it becomes a delightful game to see who can spot him first in a far-upstage tangle. This becomes almost too self-conscious, it seems to me; almost as artificial as having all the dancers line up in a deep bow as the great man enters. This is not to say that the star system has vanished from the scene—even some modern companies are reactionary in this case—but that a new use of people and a new respect for them have taken root in this part of the theater.

Therefore, in thinking specifically about a group assignment for students, this over-all belief in the individual's dignity and importance is the fundamental approach. One could compose with a solo figure, supported by some minor slaveys, but this would no longer be the norm; rather, it would be the exception. It all depends on the theme, of course, but today's notions of what to dance about rarely fall into the pattern of the queen and her obsequious courtiers, unless historical material is used. The interrelationship of forces and people in dance reflects the democratic ways of thinking, and is not only almost inescapable but imperative if we are to dance with the times. Here again I am speaking of Western, and specifically of American, attitudes. Other values and other ways obtain in far places, some of them clung to anachronistically by a stubborn few, and some unchanged from ancient days.

Before launching on an assignment for a group, I would like to point out some purely technical matters which must be kept in mind. Referring back to the design studies for two bodies, a reminder is in order that the use of more bodies indicates less complexity; more simplicity in linear design is a must. Suppose we start modestly with three or four in a group, and visually illustrate not only some relationships in space, but the fact that, with four dancers, all eight arms, eight legs, forty fingers and forty toes are going to make our group look like a centipede on the hunt if everybody move energetically at once. Vivid illustrations of bad judgment in these respects, right before the students' eyes, are so hilarious that they should make an impression that lasts forever, but, unfortunately, often it does not. Using a unit of four, I improvise some purely mathematical divisions, such as all four in unison; one against three; two and two; one dormant while the other three carry on in several ways; three dormant or as subdued accompaniment to one. These divisions are also improvised in various directions, with entrances and exits; use of stage space, as in the previous assignment; and with the always-recalled contrasts in dynamics, rhythm and phrasing. Even with necessarily very simple movement, sometimes reduced to walking or running, students will readily catch the idea, and be sufficiently prepared to undertake a group study. The whole procedure is reviewed again: start with a motivation which must have action inherent in it; try to phrase movement for a variety of relationships, and establish a beginning and an ending. In short, remember everything and apply everything learned so far to a group.

One additional matter is of the greatest importance. When the group assembles, first select a director, one who will make the final decisions. Then agree among yourselves not to allow discussion to degenerate into argument; otherwise tempers become frayed, nothing much gets done and time is wasted. Reasonably competent people should be able to put together a group study in two to three hours, or less.

A curious result of these studies occurs so often that one comes to expect it: They will all be static. Somehow, thinking about relationships stops the students from moving in space, in spite of the fact that their

WRONG

In group design, simplicity is a must

studies are full of ground-covering movement. I have various conjectures as to this. One is that the students are often crowded into small studios to work on such an assignment. Another is that with the very dramatic ideas they choose, the whole thing tends to bog down in pantomime because they have not yet had help or experience in translating their ideas into movement. Another is just plain inertia; these studies are all composed without music, so the student tends to work in his everyday living tempo and limited space functioning. He misses the stimulation of fast, accented music, and his imagination does not furnish him with a substitute. Because this happens so often, I try to issue warnings in advance. "Walk to the studio, but don't walk or sit down or stand still when you get there. A studio is a place for heightened action; resist that lethargy and that tendency to pantomime. And look for contrasts. Contrast in the theme will help, too. Pick simple opposites like aggression-timidity; lost-found; angels-devils; questions-answers." There are thousands of ideas of this sort

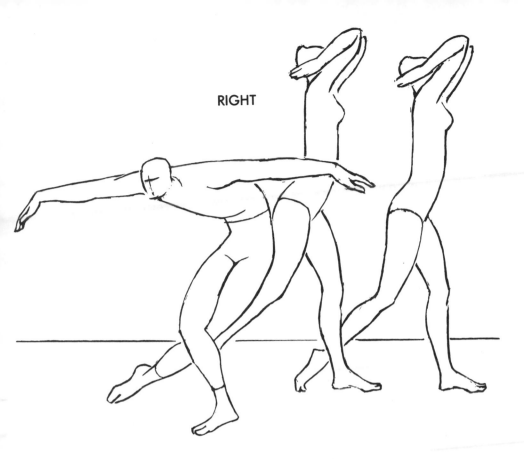

RIGHT

which are better to start with than the pretentious ones students sometimes bring in, such as "A Dictator and His Slaves," "A Crumbling Society," or "Lucrezia Borgia and Her Relatives." Big ideas and meager equipment are not very good mates.

When these studies are ready, I call for accompaniment, and what this should be is a matter for discussion. The expert piano accompanist is usually the best solution, but other sounds should be considered, such as percussion, vocal chanting or singing and sound effects. These afford a fine opportunity to open the young minds to the sensitive fitting together of accompaniment and movement; and were there time, many hours of experimentation along these lines would be most rewarding.

A group work, even a short study, is very difficult at this stage, and patience is in order. I find that students cannot cope with and remember many of the points of the previous lessons. Design, for instance, is often too symmetrical, and therefore static. Or projection is missing (they throw away the movement), or the phrasing is fuzzy, or the dynamics are monotonous. They need words of encouragement and hope at this point, when it all seems impossibly difficult, and what they thought was going to be fun turns out to be hard work. Classes in choreography, like emotional people, are subject to depressions, and about here a mood of severe discouragement and frustration sets in, which calls for a definite lift in morale. If the teacher fails in this, a sure cure is to call in a few visitors and show the best studies of the class to date. A successful performance is everybody's restorative, and matters should then continue with renewed spirit and courage.

Assignment

Bring in a group study for three or four.

Dynamics

11 Dynamics is the ingredient which adds spice and interest to living as well as dancing. There is not a nook or cranny of the physical world as we know it that does not have some variety in texture. In painting this would be surface texture, color and intensity; in music, timbre plus loud, soft, legato, and staccato; in movement, smooth and sharp plus gradations in tension. I think of dynamics as a scale extending from the smoothness of cream to the sharpness of a tack hammer. And the whole scale is subject to endless variations in tempo and tension: slow-smooth with force; fast-smooth without tension; fast-sharp with tension (like pistol shots), moderate-sharp with little force (rather blunt), slow-smooth without tension (dreamy, sluggish or despairing) and so forth. (See first photo following for example of subtle dynamics; second photo for example of sharper dynamic contrast.)

Life offers endless examples of our appetite for dynamic interests. Interior decorators work tirelessly to provide the contrasts which transform a room from drab to stunning. The over-all color scheme is of great concern, textures a source of endless effort, and just the right accent—say, the blue T'ang Dynasty horse—is chosen with loving care. Even the least aesthetic people like variety in the taste of food, in the color of clothes, in entertainment, in kinds of people and conversation. An undynamic civilization would really be quite unbearable, and almost too difficult to imagine. It is easy to believe that members of such an unfortunate segment of the human race would die of boredom. Here again, Americans are more restless and more demanding of variety than most; they are a fast, nervous nation which likes everything shorter, spicier, more jolting and in vast quantities.

In working for an awareness of dynamics in a group of students, we must first take note of the fact that the words sharp, smooth, fast, slow, tension, relaxation are all relative terms, subject to individual interpretation according to the personality make-up of the dancer. In the moderately fast, easygoing dancer with natural co-ordination, "sharp" does not reach a normal pitch of intensity. But in the onlooker there is an unconscious and accurate evaluation of the scale of dynamics. He knows what is sharp and what is smooth when he looks at it, but when called on to produce this scale, he is often so much the prisoner of his physical self that he cannot deliver it. There are difficult cases, especially in regard to sharpness. This dynamic is the result of the ability to command quick applications of energy plus speed. Almost everybody can be smooth and slow. Fast people can be slowed down, and the majority are in the moderate-tempo dynamic class anyhow, but to sharpen moderate and slow people takes considerable patience and training. Too often I have to say over and over, "That's not sharp, it only feels so to you."

Another point which must be learned is the proper choice of move-ment to deliver the smooth or fast-sharp dynamic. In regard to sharp, the body, except for that of the virtuoso, is not naturally built to make just any movement staccato. For instance, circular movement in general cannot be made to look sharp, because the very nature of the curve is smooth and continuous. This would apply to the turn as well as to circular movement of, especially, the big joints. Swings from the shoulder, or of the legs from the hip, are impossible to sharpen. They cannot be fast enough, first of all, nor do they have any points of accent. Movement of this kind can only be sharpened by segmentation—that is, by breaking up the course of the curve with accented thrusts. For example, a swing from the hip can be broken up or added to by sharp accents of the knee or the foot. The turn itself, often very fast, feels terrifically sharp to the dancer if he is whizzing around, but the mere revolving is curving and legato, and does not look sharp except when something else is added, like the thrust of the arm, body or leg. This is the secret of the famous fouetté turn of the ballet; it's that sharp knee moving in and out which gives it brilliance. As a contrast, the turn à la seconde is not nearly so exciting because it is all smooth.

It is axiomatic that sharp dynamics plus speed is stimulating and that smooth plus moderate or slow is soothing. The good choreographer never stays very long with any one dynamic because he very well knows that too much sharp wears out the nervous system, and too much legato puts everybody to sleep. In this respect, however, the student has to have his judgment tuned up so that it responds to the treasure of dynamics like a

Geiger counter. Studies are devised for this to give him practice in manipulating dynamics.

An assistant shows a sequence of movement done successively in four different dynamics. It is short, consisting of three or four phrases, and it is repeated exactly the same each time. First it is all smooth and slow. Care must be taken to choose movement which will be possible to sharpen later on, remembering that not all movement is suitable for this. Big circular designs of the arms, legs or body are almost impossible to sharpen. In general, thrusting movements and those of the smaller parts of the body are the most practical. Now this sequence is done all sharp, which means with fast accents, but not necessarily in an increased tempo. Pauses can be introduced between the movements to keep the phrases approximately the same length. Ask the class to note the difference in the mood and meaning conveyed by these two approaches. The first will be calm, probably poetic, certainly not impassioned, since it has a minimal tension. The second is notable immediately for its aggressiveness and feeling; emotion is at work, especially if considerable energy is added to the sharp timing. The movements, though the same, take on an entirely different meaning.

Thirdly, the sequence is done with alternate dynamics, some smooth, some sharp. Because of the nature of the production of these movements, there will be a variety in timing as well as dynamics. It takes time to be smooth. The eye must follow a certain line long enough to register its quality, but the sharp must always be fast. This combination sequence makes a different effect. I would say this is the norm. The alternate dynamics are rich in interest, and refreshing. This is the most likable area of communication. We are pleased, for instance, by voices which have these contrasts, by clothing which is "slow," worn with accessories which are "fast and sharp," or at least show variety in color and texture. We like these things in painting, ceramics, fabrics, music, drama and dancing, not to mention just living.

There is one more process for our phrase to go through, and this is simultaneous dynamics. This will probably mean adding a little material to the original so that the contrasts will be clear. For instance, if the theme is in the arms, one arm can continue as before, while the other beats or quivers. This could be endlessly varied by uses of other parts of the body.

The feet can be staccato while the arms and body are legato, and so forth. This is also very pleasing, though much more complex, and produces a very rich mixture. One example of this sort of thing, which is age-old, is the Spanish dance. How well they know that those sinuous, sensuous arms can be combined with exciting heel beats. Good tap dancing is another example of almost the same technique, but it is utterly different in style. This is not, obviously, the result of any thought on the part of the Spaniard or the tap dancer, who established their technical means by a complicated combination of environment and temperament—which would be fascinating to trace, but which certainly did not include analysis. The early modern dancers were without a tradition; they all had to invent their own, and naturally arrived at some conclusions which had already been discovered by instinct hundreds of years before. Some of the very familiar ideas, like the smooth and sharp of the Spanish dance, can, however, be used in principle in new ways, and behold, they are fresh ideas clothed in the tried and true colors of ancient times.

Dynamics is the lifeblood of the dance, and is ignored at the peril of your existence as an artist. At this point in the lessons, I like to say that every dancer has certain predilections, areas which are *simpatico* to his temperament, and which he will tend to move in habitually. Dynamic contrast may be one of these, but it is rarely the dominant characteristic. In this case, he must cultivate it with ardor until it becomes quite impossible for him to move with monotonous texture. Every dancer has some kind of movement in which he feels particularly at home. To some, this would be slow-smooth, or with emphasis on design, or on drama, or on technique. It is the obligation of the teacher to try to dig him out of his grooves, and set him adventuring on new paths. In not more than one lesson, I can readily see that that one always moves in a big, heroic way; this one is always vague and indecisive; another is small and frightened. To the heroic girl I say, "Do something funny, make me laugh." To the timid, "Pretend you are Genghis Khan." To the lethargic, "Be fast, like streaks of lightning." This is uncomfortable, even dismaying, for them; it is quite devastating to be thrown out of the nest and told to fly. Nevertheless, stringent measures are in order if we are to enlarge the range.

A. Assignment

Bring a dynamic study for one body, a sequence of movement to be done in four ways: all smooth, all sharp, alternating smooth and sharp, and simultaneously smooth and sharp.

B. Assignment

Bring a duet, trio or quartet with its emphasis on dynamics.

If there is time, these are assigned in successive lessons; otherwise the class is divided and each group given one assignment to work on at the same time.

The group project calls for further explanation, in any case. Referring back to the first design assignment, the procedure is much the same. The solo instrument is all-inclusive, but the group or duet immediately requires a divison of the material between its members. In the dynamic assignment, try to pick subject matter which will naturally suggest contrasting dynamics and simultaneous or alternating dynamics between members of a group. For instance, patience-impatience, friendliness-coldness, earth-bound against air-borne. Also, warn against too much contrast. This can be very wearing, too, and the relief of unison movement, all in one quality, is a welcome contrast in itself. Advise the class that larger groups and a study of over-all form will come in due time.

Rhythm

12 Of all the ingredients in the art of the dance, rhythm is the most persuasive and most powerful element, with the possible exception of virtuoso technique and dazzling personality. Where design is striking, rhythm is rousing, and dynamics is a subtle coloring compared to a driving rhythm. But rhythm is also one of the least used and least appreciated tools in the dance. All the major forms of dance—ballet, ethnic and modern—stress other factors much more, such as technique (those higher extensions and faster turns), drama, originality, purity in the medium, charm and personality or style, and endless other facets of the diamond that glitters across the footlights. The people who really know the worth of rhythm are the tap and jazz dancers. Experts in the field have built castles in Spain, complete with Hollywood swimming pools—all on practically nothing but rhythm. Why this indifference exists in the field in general I really do not know, but at every opportunity I stress the glories and the excitement of rhythm and urge students not to throw away this treasure.

Rhythm so permeates every aspect of human beings, and indeed, of the known world, that it might be compared to the ambience of existence, like the water in which the fish moves, the water and the fish having rhythmical differentials, too, of which each is quite unaware. . . . Or are they? The currents and the tides certainly speak to the fish in primeval and instinctive ways, and who can say that water does not respond to the fish in some mysterious sense because of his swimming and darting? It is tempting to be almost mystical about rhythm, as time after time the uses, absences, withdrawals and distortions of rhythm are observed to affect profoundly the ways of everything from men to atoms. Rhythm is the great organizer. Habits of accent form to hold an organism together, patterns of rhythmical shape lend sense and sensibility to life, and the un-rhythmical mass of matter is anarchistic, chaotic, a menace to all organization.

Coming to problems of rhythm in dance, every director and teacher

knows the arhythmic individual who has so imperfect a co-ordination between the ear and the body that he cannot conform to a beat, is out of
step with everybody, aims for an accent half a beat later than he should,
and in general is hopeless rhythmically. For my part I find this such
a handicap, and so disrupting and exasperating to deal with, that I cannot
make use of arhythmic people in my compositions. This is a particularly
acute problem with me because I am so aware of, and so in love with,
rhythm. With another director, who does not stress this element, or whose
method allows for individual timings, irrespective of an established beat,
unrhythmical dancers would get along very nicely. Quite often these
dancers have a strong personal sense of timing, which, although they cannot make it conform to any other pattern, is highly sensitive and even
exciting.

To go into a full-scale inquiry into rhythm would require a book in
itself, and would lead from the minutiae of matter through evolution,
with all its flora and fauna, to man; and beyond that—conjecture. But in a
book of dance we will start several hundred million years after the beginning with that extraordinary production of nature—man. He has four
sources of rhythmical organization. First, the breathing-singing-speaking
apparatus which leads to phrasing, and phrase rhythm. Then the partly unconscious rhythms of function: the heartbeat, peristalsis, contraction and
relaxation of muscles, waves of sensation through the nerve ends. Another,
is the propelling mechanism, the legs, which man discovered would support him, one after the other, while moving in space, and which provided
also a conscious joy in beat as the weight changed. Lastly, there is
emotional rhythm: surges and ebbs of feeling, with accents which not
only supply strong rhythmical patterns but are a measure for judging
emotional rhythms in others. If I feel these tides of passion, then all
other men must feel them too, in some degree.

For dancers, the motor mechanism is certainly the most important.
Here is where the original dance began—with the feet—and here is where
it still carries on, in the main. Not only that, but I think the awareness of
accent, energy punctuated by beat, stems only from this change of weight
in dance, and would not exist in music or language or visual arts had it
not been established by the feet of men. Think what the world would be
if it were inhabited by superfishes instead of supermonkeys. Accent would
be absent or meaningless. Rhythm would have no beat because the fish has

none; the fins are in a legato rhythm. All its movement, no matter how quick, is not really sharp in the sense of a footstep, but sinuous and smooth. There would never have been a clock—because the hours are beats in time—no drums, and no love of noisy accents anywhere. A parade of marching fishes would be impossible, it would instead be an undulating advance with no drum major. But possibly it would be much more beautiful and easier on the nerves.

Thinking further about the rhythms of change of weight, the mechanism of the walk consists of a balance on one leg while the other is lifted and advanced by the muscles. As the descent of this leg begins, force is no longer necessary. Gravity takes over, and the foot strikes the surface with only a braking action, which results in the familiar "footfall." This down stroke can be emphasized and reinforced by energy so that it is very heavy indeed, like the turn of the English palace guard, or it can be controlled and softened, with the toe substituting for the heel, as in dancing. Nevertheless, it is gravity which provides the beat potential. Referring to fishes once more, gravity plays so little part in their activity that up and down motion hardly exists, and their attenion is fastened to progression easily supported by water. In the human animal, the walk is the key pattern of fall and recovery, my theory of motion—that is, the giving in to and rebound from gravity. This is the very core of all movement, in my opinion. All life fluctuates between the resistance to and the yielding to gravity. Youth is "down" as little as possible; gravity holds him lightly to earth. Old age gradually takes over and the spring vanishes from the step until the final yielding, death. There are two still points in the physical life: the motionless body, in which the thousand adjustments for keeping it erect are invisible, and the horizontal, the last stillness. Life and dance exist between these two points and therefore form the arc between two deaths. This lifetime span is filled with thousands of falls and recoveries—all highly specialized and exaggerated in the dance—which result in accents of all qualities and timings. If these movements, especially of the feet, augmented by other parts of the body, are organized into rhythmic patterns, they are connected as by an umbilical cord to everybody's life. The more speed and bounce they have, the more youth and vitality are suggested and remembered. The more weak and sparse the up accents, the older and less dynamic they seem. This is not to suggest that youth is good and old age is bad, but is merely a clinical observation as to the way these impressions of young and old arise rhythmically.

Not only is the rise and fall, energy versus gravity pattern embedded in every move of all men, but the dancer has the privilege of tapping one of the most potent aspects of this life motion when he organizes it into rhythms. Everybody responds to a beat, and to a complex one at that, as long as he is able to discern the pattern. It has been noted before, though it is largely unexplainable, that man likes to understand things in terms of shape, and is unaffected, or downright unhappy, when confronted with anything of which he does not understand the pattern. In dance and music, the arts which make the most conscious use of rhythm, understanding of the keynote of the rhythmic organization enhances enjoyment no end. People are not carried along with the hit-or-miss or too-erratic accent. This kind of enjoyment seems to be related to relaxation and effort. If the rhythmic structure is perceived, then a constant effort of the will is not needed to understand it, hence more ease and more pleasure result than if a jumble of accent were presented which was difficult to follow, with the consequent need for close attention and an expenditure of nervous energy. We like the unexpected in rhythm, too. How well the jazz dancers and musicians know that. Against a "solid" background of steady beat, it becomes delightful and comprehensible. This sort of "beat" rhythm is only one part of the subject, however—the division I call motor rhythm. The other two—breath rhythm and emotional rhythm—are extremely potent, too.

The breath rhythm does not have the excitement of the beat, since by its very nature it is not primarily concerned with the physical lift and drop of the feet. Moreover, the ordinary breath has no sharp accent inherent in it. Nevertheless, it is tied to the most vital instinct in man; the newborn child struggles to breathe and to live, and the dying cling to breathing as the connecting link with survival. In the dance we can use the simple rise and fall of the breath in its original location in the chest, but this is by no means all. The idea of breath rhythm—the inhalation, the suspension and the exhalation—can be transferred to other parts of the body. One can "breathe" with the knees, or the arms, or the whole body. This transference will not seem artificial, but miraculously natural and satisfying. The feet, though they play a part in this kind of rhythm, will serve mainly to carry the body unobtrusively from one breath to another. These breath rhythms are subject to the most infinite variety as to parts of the body, shorter and longer timing, and various uses of space. In other words, there is a whole world of movement implicit in just this part of rhythm. But, like motor rhythms, it is so neglected by dancers, teachers and choreographers that in class work I have considerable difficulty in merely making students understand it, and one seldom sees either rhythm in finished compositions.

The emotional rhythm is in more universal use, however. Almost everybody likes to be dramatic, and in some quarters this is the end-all and be-all of composition. The emotional rhythm may be cast into a breath rhythm, a motor rhythm or gesture sequences. It is subject to many manipulations and combinations with other factors. If used properly, its chief characteristic is its truth. It must convince us that its roots are in reality. It must avoid being so artificial that we are unmoved. Secondly, it is never in a monotone, as the human being is not capable of sustaining a feeling in an absolutely steady intensity and rhythm. Here it differs radically from the other two. Motor rhythms can be, if called for, absolutely metronomic, and breath rhythms can rise and fall steadily and be related to the original function. But emotion, by its very nature, fluctuates; hence the dramatic rhythmic pattern must show variation if it is to be convincing. To be fully prepared to work on emotional rhythms, students will have to complete the analysis of motivation and gesture, which is the last of the compositional elements to be inquired into.

While we are considering rhythm, it is appropriate to look into some very curious aspects of tempo. I will ask a class, "Tell me, how do you determine when slow becomes moderate, and moderate becomes fast?" In other words, fast is faster than what, not in terms of names for these tempi but in terms of movement? Sometimes I get what I consider the right answer—that the measure for tempo is the rate of normal walking (not the heartbeat, although this is a contributing factor). I then institute some experiments. An assistant moves at various walking and running speeds. All the students invariably agree when it is slow, moderate, fast or very fast; there seems to be a built-in timer in this respect. The normal estimate of tempo can be altered artificially by starting a dance at a brisk speed and increasing this to presto, so that the original opening seems moderate by comparison. Tempi, therefore, are relative to each other as well. Slow and fast, as related to the walk, have psychological effects. Slower than the normal pace is always more lethargic, even though it is thoughtful; faster is always more exciting, exhilarating, indicating a quickened desire and increased vitality. The moderate pace, the workaday tempo, is always rather chancy, too familiar to be stimulating, neither exciting nor profound. To combine this grey area with some other, similar ones, I warn against too much of the moderate pace, too much symmetry, too-even rhythm accents, too much horizontal design, and so forth. In short, stay away from the deadly middle.

Assignments are now given out for studies in the three rhythms, beginning with the single body. If these ideas are particularly unfamiliar, it may take considerable illustration by an assistant to prepare students to work by themselves. There are usually two or three who are woefully unrhythmic in a metric sense, and who are advised to make an intensive study of musical and body rhythms elsewhere. Often they have never heard of breath rhythm before, and emotional rhythms mean to them gesticulation and pantomine. Nevertheless, we plunge into the subject, and make progress according to the experience of the class.

Assignment

Bring in a study illustrating a motor rhythm, a breath rhythm and an emotional rhythm for one body.

Motivation and Gesture

13 A movement without a motivation is unthinkable. Some force is the cause for change of position, whether it is understandable or not. This applies not just to dancing, but to the physical world in general. Choreographers can and do ignore motivation, making no explanation to themselves or others, but try as they may to be abstract, they cannot avoid saying, "I live, therefore I move!" The cessation of movement is death, but before that the dancer at least makes the minimal statement, "I am a live human being." The only way I can think of to avoid this is to encase the body in a sort of box costume in which no part of the anatomy shows, and nothing reveals a living muscle underneath. Anybody want to try this? It might really be an abstraction, as it would be cause for conjecture whether a human being inhabited the outfit, or a mechanism. Even here motivation is at work; someone must have been inspired to invent the mechanism.

Obviously I am for conscious motivation, and therefore in favor of communication about people to people. I insist from the beginning of class work, and with professional dancers, too, that movement should be supported by a purpose, even that no move be made until a reason, simple as it may be, demands it. This procedure should prevent the technical, cold, mechanical performance, because feeling will be present. Even the technical dance has a motivation, of course. It says, "I am an expert with my body and I will dazzle you with physical prowess." Once in a great while this is valid, and we can enjoy the communication of a real virtuoso. But this kind of thing really comes in the category of tricks and acrobatics, and is hardly within the purlieu of art unless accompanied by faultless aesthetic taste.

To me, the really dull and unforgivable dance is the performance by the mediocre technician, who has nothing to say beyond the mere fact of being alive. If the choreographer has been able to infuse his work with some fresh movement ideas, the emptiness of it will be somewhat mitigated; otherwise we are in for real starvation. This is particularly true of today, because practically every dancer setting foot on a stage has a technique ranging from adequate to brilliant. If it is in the service of nothing, nothing will result except the awareness that everybody has technique. Such is the avidity of dancers and the expertise of teachers that they can all dance, and well; technicians are a dime a dozen. For my taste, something must be added to make this display worth while, and that something is motivation.

To draw a brief comparison with drama, the sister art of the dance, no playwright I ever heard of has written an "abstract" drama with words put together at random, and characters entering and exiting with no purpose. Dramatists can be very difficult to understand, but almost without exception they are trying to say something, and would think it quite absurd to put into the mouths of the actors "me-me-me" and "ah-ah-ah" from the diction textbook. Parlor tricks involving actors who recite from the telephone book are known for what they are—party games. I consider dance to be firmly in the area of communication. It is making a mistake when it takes on the more abstract elements of music and painting, which are totally different arts, with a human being once removed from the core of the performance. The dancer's medium is the· body, not paint or stone or sound.

In teaching motivation in choreographic classes, a great deal of spadework has to be done. This is because the background of technical training is so extremely limited. There is one dominant, unspoken goal that exists among members of a technique class. They all want to achieve a mythical ideal—that of a youth, male or female, not more than twenty years old, with perfect physical co-ordination, supple, strong, healthy, happy, confident, beautiful, not subject to nerves or depression or fatigue. As a background for progression into a dance-drama, a piece of work calling for a range of experience and emotion, this standard is fantastically unrealistic. The dancer has not the faintest notion how to look discouraged or bewildered or shocked emotionally. I myself have never been able to direct certain dancers so that they will convey convincingly desperate fatigue or a longing despair. They simply have no idea where these things lie in the body; nor can they be stimulated to optimistic heights of ecstasy. Paroxysms of joy are not included in technical training; the happy youth does not go to extremes but lives in that reasonable rosy paradise of the moderate ideal. Incidentally, there should be a class in the technique of expressing emotional states long before students reach the performing or choreographing stage. It must be noted that a few teachers employ emotional movement; in fact it is embedded right in the technique. But these movements, when they do occur, are invariably very limited, usually derived from the personal whims of the originator and are not nearly broad enough to serve as a technical foundation. I ask young dancers how a baby walks, or what happens to the body in terms of posture and movement in old age, and they are at a complete loss, even though they have seen babies and old people all their lives. They look, but they do not see. Or I ask, "If despair begins to creep over you, where will the first indication be, and after that, what parts of the body will follow?" They don't know. So, to deal with motivation, which ranges very far from the happy ideal, the students must take a close look at the natural reactions of themselves and other people, and exercises have to be fairly prolonged before any studies in motivated movement or gesture are undertaken.

Motivation is the all-inclusive core of dance composition, and gesture is a branch of it. To make this difference clear, let us start with motivation, and then compare it to gesture. The urge to move may spring from the most tenuous and gossamer source, all delicacy and fragility in its origin, but still strong enough to make something happen. For instance, an almost lethargic curiosity can move one finger, or just the eyes. This can be complicated further by a coloring emotion, say of furtiveness, suspicion or hope. Students should experiment with these mutations and, incidentally, become aware of the power of the small movement. They are all too prone to exercise vast energy in the use of the whole body, and never think of isolating various parts of it for expressive purposes. These early studies are much like acting, but so be it. The original natural sources of emotion must be explored, and the process by which emotions are turned from mime into movement must be examined subsequently.

I devise various exercises by way of setting up simple situations, for which the students choose the movements. For example: You are very disturbed by some emotional problem, but after wrestling with it briefly, you make a decision, either to face and conquer it, or to run away or otherwise conclude it. This little study has, in microscopic size, a great deal to teach the young student. In the first place, how will he indicate emotional disturbance? To understand this in a small assignment is to have a guide toward similar problems forever. Deeply felt emotion always begins in the middle body, where the heart, the lungs and the viscera respond immediately and first. Other reactions may follow very swiftly, so as to seem simultaneous.

The hands may fly to any of those parts, or to the head, or be clasped close to the body, and so forth. Also, reactions of the head, legs and other parts of the body may follow. These would depend on the nature of the feeling. If it is a sudden shock, the hands will go to the breast or the heart, where an immediate, violent increase in tension is going on; or to the head or eyes, if the emotion involves a wish to shut out the painful sensation, or if weeping is indicated. If this feeling is not sharp, like a shock, but a gradual realization, reaction will still come first in the middle body, as always, but may be accompanied by more peripheral movement, such as rollings and liftings of the head, claspings or beatings of the hands against some outside object, or restless movements of the feet. The one procedure that would be psychologically incorrect would be to maintain the pulled-up diaphragm and the erect, beautiful carriage of the classroom. This is for opera singers, who can't very well suffer in a collapsed position of the lungs and diaphragm.

The student should be asked to think specifically about his emotional state, not just indulge in vague agonizing. What is the cause? Has your lover deserted you, or have you lost your handbag? Entirely different sets of movements are indicated, depending on the subject matter. This, of course, should be related to previous studies as well; it should have a phrase, and all the rest of it.

Then we come to the decision. We must see it in unmistakable terms. I find this a particularly difficult moment for dancers to cope with. Because they are trained to think in terms of movement, they are apt to react much too rapidly, leaving out the intermediate stages, and merely state the *fait accompli.* Suppose the idea is defiance of trouble. From carrying on in mortal agony with elaborate detail, the dancer will suddenly straighten up with a high chest, in his full strength of youth and courage. This is so unconvincing as to verge on the comic. The intermediate stages of coming to a decision, the gradual cessation of suffering, no matter how brief, must be there or we cannot believe in the idea. The patterns for all this are embedded in life, and in the dancer, but he has scarcely noticed what goes on, being so immersed in acquiring a technique for posture, beauty, perfect co-ordination, etc., etc. The psychologists tell us that strongly felt emotion has an instant reaction in the middle body, and this is true of either dark or happy feelings. In these early stages, the studies will be fairly pantomimic, but we ignore this as long as there is a true understanding of motivation-movement. Although this is so similar to acting, there is yet one vast difference. The actor has words.

To illustrate the tremendous difference between the dancer or the mime, who must say everything with the body alone, and the word-actor, consider the point in the study at which the decision is made. The actor can stand in a semicollapsed position or subtle state of suffering, and say without moving a muscle, "No, I won't," and the scene will be ended there. But the dancer must make the "no" explicit and visible in movement, and not in the fast timing of words, which can eliminate transitions by suggestion.

Many studies of a similar nature are most useful, and are only limited by time. Also, of course, this sort of emotional training can be carried on in rehearsals of a dance work. But to cope with motivated movement at all, in composition, the students must have some help on emotional training in class work. One of the most notable effects of motivation in movement is its power to co-ordinate. The dancer, when he is really suffused with feeling of which he understands most of the import, will be "all of a piece." That is, no one part of the body will be out of line, so as to make it necessary to control or alter it by a conscious effort. This is a great saving of energy, but it will happen only if the dancer is able to find the real roots of emotional behavior and wrap himself in them. This sort of thing is obviously not just a classroom study, to be pigeonholed and forgotten, but is a challenge to the dancer throughout his composing and professional life. There is always more to be learned about it in regard to each new role or composition—unless he's going to devote himself to the flowers and the butterflies. Along the way I have often been obliged to teach young men how to make love, and young girls how to be predatory or flirtatious or seductive, and I've had to advise everybody how to express anxiety, alarm and endless other emotional states. They may have felt these things, but the movements for them are like complete strangers.

As a branch or division of motivation, I also explore with students what I refer to as gesture. This is easier because gestures are patterns of movement established by long usage among men, a sort of language of communication or function which has been going on since the beginning of time, and which is most useful because it is so recognizable. I divide gesture into four categories: social, functional, ritual and emotional. In each of these areas people have crystallized movement into patterns, some of which are so highly stylized and remote from their origins that it takes thought and ingenuity to track down the original movement. In taking these up, one at a time, in the order in which they are studied, I begin with:

Social Gesture

Some examples follow, shown by an assistant: the bow, the handshake, the farewell, the embrace (from formal to intimate), the salute. Then there are situations such as the parade, the baseball game, both players and audience, the party, the reception, the political rally, the public speech. All of these have well-known gestures which, if even touched upon, communicate their meanings at once, and are grist for the movement mill of the dancer.

To go into detail about just one of them, consider the bow and its fascinating evolution. Today it is often a corruption of the original, just a movement of the hand somewhere near the head—and this is a very faint reminder, indeed, of what it was. I imagine the following sequence in the history of the bow. Originally it was a prostration of the captured enemy, face down, hands out, before the throne of a conqueror. The body was in a defenseless position, exposing the vulnerable back of the neck; was innocent of concealed weapons because of the exposed hands. The captive was totally at the whim and will of his captor. Note that the ordination of cardinals in the Catholic Church and worship in Hindu temples still call for this abject submission. Along the way somewhere the captive was thrown to his knees, instead of flat down. Very likely this was quicker when a great many were to be dealt with; their hands were tied behind them, but the bodies were well bent down, the backs of the necks still exposed, the heads bare. This was also the position of worship in many primitive religions. Now, to hurry past several hundred years of development, we come to the court and the era of the knight and the courtier. By this time our supplicant is on one knee only, has removed his hat with a great flourish and a sweeping body movement involving a step back with the feet. Perhaps he is being knighted. His ruler places the blade of his sword along the bare neck and utters the appropriate words, after which the newly honored backs away from the monarch, bent forward in the age-old position of submission and respect. In the courts of the French, English and Italian kings the bow became a very elaborate affair indeed—and any drama school worth its salt sees to it that students know the etiquette of the court bow—but it still retained its salient characteristics, the bare head, the bent and exposed neck. Even in the most casual use of the bow, as between friends, it never lost the traces of these two ideas. Later on this was to be corrupted so that men merely raised their hats on informal occasions, and finally the last degeneration, the mere touching of a finger to an often nonexistent hat brim.

In using some form of the bow in a dance, the merest indication of its inclination from the body and lowered head will set the whole association of its meaning alive in the eye of the beholder. This would also be true of the greeting, the farewell, the embrace; in fact, of a hundred social gestures. The dancer can call on these movements to serve him; they are like well-known words for which he has no need to invent a substitute. In fact, he cannot, as nothing says bow except bow.

Functional Gesture

Movements which have been developed for practical use exist by the thousands, and these gestures can be taken away from their original environment and made use of in the art of movement. Referring back to a part of the design assignment, one of the subjects for this was work. This involves functional gesture. There are dozens of these movements which should occur to the student choreographer, and he should be made aware that they are useful "words" which can be fitted into a composition, not only when a plot line specifically indicates "workers," but in more abstract situations where effort is indicated. They are like short cuts to composition. An already-made set of movements for work—say, carrying a heavy burden —will not only provide the pattern for symbolic burdens, but will insure muscular effort in the right places. Also, these practical sources make movement more specific, which is highly desirable, I think, in the face of much obscure, vague moving around. When confronted with a passage in which a dancer has both arms extended straight to the side, palms down, and one leg up and forward, I am astonished to hear, on inquiry, that this means, "I am carrying the burden of my guilt."

To express the essence of work, the dance movement must contain certain characteristics which are embedded in the original action. Very few kinds of functional effort require full extensions of the whole body, or even any of its parts. Leverage, used in innumerable tasks, calls for bent knees and elbows, arms and hands which do not go to the end of their reach, and, in general, tension directed to a focus from a firmly leg-balanced body.

Random examples of functional gesture would be: combing hair, rocking a baby, sawing wood, scrubbing a floor, sleeping, sewing, dressing, walking, running (with an objective, such as catching a bus), typing, signing a letter. If these sound dreadfully prosaic to the dancer who has his mind fastened on a poetic dream of beauty, it seems to me that it will do him a world of good to come down from the rainbow and live temporarily in reality. Mundane as the above examples are, they can be and have been —after their magical bath of stylization—very useful in composition, often yielding movement which would otherwise never be thought of.

Ritual Gesture

Ritual seems to have all but disappeared from the modern world; but when one looks closely, there is a good deal left. In any case, in our search for gesture, we are free to roam over all of history, and back to the conjectures of pre-recorded time. The ancient world was obviously full of ritual. Historians tell us that the early Hindu and the Greek of classical time were so busy with the formal aspects of their religious life that they had very little time for anything else. There is an enormous amount of primitive ritual which still exists. Nowadays we have well-established movements connected with a wide variety of religions; there are also other semisocial ritualistic occasions, such as the procedures in a court of law, the crowning of a monarch, the inauguration of a high official, a political nominating session. The beauty of tapping these sources is that they have the value of directness. One could contrive, I suppose, an entirely original design for worship, but why strain to do this when one can "tune in" on a movement, the implications of which everybody recognizes at once.

One very curious factor calls for comment in respect to the bow of social use, and the bow of religious ritual. The bare head for the male is *de rigueur* on social occasions, but not in some churches or, notably, in the synagogue, where the orthodox, both men and women, cover their heads. In Catholic and high Protestant faiths the woman's head must be covered, but not the man's. These are not whims, but have very good reasons for existing as they do. Also the bow, or genuflection, of the church has common roots with the social bow; it has the drop of the head and the forward body, but it is different in degree. These alterations are worthy of keen observation and filing away in the archives of the dancer's vocabulary.

Emotional Gesture

No category of gesture is more useful to the dancer or more extensive than this one. Nevertheless, the strictly patterned gestures of emotional states, those so often occurring as to be easily readable, are not so numerous as one might think. There are many feelings which can be expressed in so many ways that there really is no one pattern for them. For example, hope has no shape, nor do inspiration, fear or love. They have characteristics, yes, but that is quite different from an established pattern. Antique mime, in drama and opera, did establish some rules as to movement for various communications. The love yearnings of Pierrot, for instance, were well established and taught as a style of acting, and the hands clasped to the heart with the body flung to the knee is still a cliché of old-fashioned drama and opera. These patterns, and many like them, are too dated and worn out to be useful nowadays to the dancer, or to any but the stylist or the satirist.

There are a few emotional states which are patterned. For instance, grief. The body will be concave. The arms will be clasped around the torso, or, if there is weeping, the hands will be at the face and eyes. There will also be a side-to-side or forward-and-back rocking motion of the body, and sobs and breathing distortions. This pattern has such strong physiological reasons for being that the gestures have crystallized through the ages. Any movement which comes near these characteristics will suggest lamenting or grieving. Only in the movies does the heroine sit bolt upright, staring into the camera, with the tears falling from her beautiful eyes. Woman in her natural state is fairly doubled up in crying spells, often flung down on a bed and using a handkerchief to wipe away the tears and blow her nose. Much too unglamorous for the pictures! In dance we never aim to be realistic either, but rather to keep roots alive and feeding on natural behavior.

Other patterned emotions can be observed better in children than in adults, who are corrupted in their actions by overdoses of etiquette. Joy, for instance, is invariably accompanied in children by jumping up and down, and sometimes spinning around. Their elders are much too dignified for this. Caution and mischievous intent walk on the toes; alarm shocks body in a short spasm, opens the eyes wide and is followed by a swift retreat into hiding. Bravado swaggers and assumes aggressive positions, elbows away from the body, chest and head well up. Intention of cruelty drops the head, concaves the chest, narrows the eyes, makes the knees bent and furtive. All these reactions have been pretty much refined in adults, so that, for instance, cruelty may only narrow the eyes, or bravado may be transferred entirely to words.

It is axiomatic that every emotion has a concomitant movement, and it is the business of the dancer and the choreographer to find out what these movements are in the specific problem at hand; they will only be convincing if they bear the mark of truth.

At this point, when considerable inquiry into natural emotional states has been going on, some of the material must be used as an example of the process of stylization away from the natural, and the turning of gesture into movement. For this I use the handshake, one of the social gestures. With the help of an assistant, I first illustrate the familiar clasp of hands of two friends meeting again, or even polite people meeting for the first time. This is in a calm, merely cordial mood, no overtones of, "Maybe this is the love of my life," or "Imagine meeting him here." The class is asked to analyze the ingredients of the handshake in regard to the four elements of movement (design, dynamics, rhythm and motivation). The handshake, like every other movement, has all four, and although individual variation exists, there is a common denominator in the use of the elements which one can call normal. The design is right angle, symmetrical, going forward, up and down and back. The dynamics—medium sharp with a decrease to smooth. The rhythm is metric and roughly a half note and several quarters, and the motivation is friendly. This is indicated by a slight forward tipping of the middle body, which always means a warmth of feeling. The phrase has a high point toward the end, during the staccato beat of the handclasp. Students should be able to "read" all this in the light of past lessons, and interpret the meaning by purely technical deduction. The right-angle, symmetrical design means strength tempered with emotional equilibrium; the moderate dynamics and unsyncopated rhythm are calm and unexcited; the middle body shows warmth and feeling but not passion; the phrase is pleasantly asymmetrical.

Now begins a series of alterations and manipulations of this material.

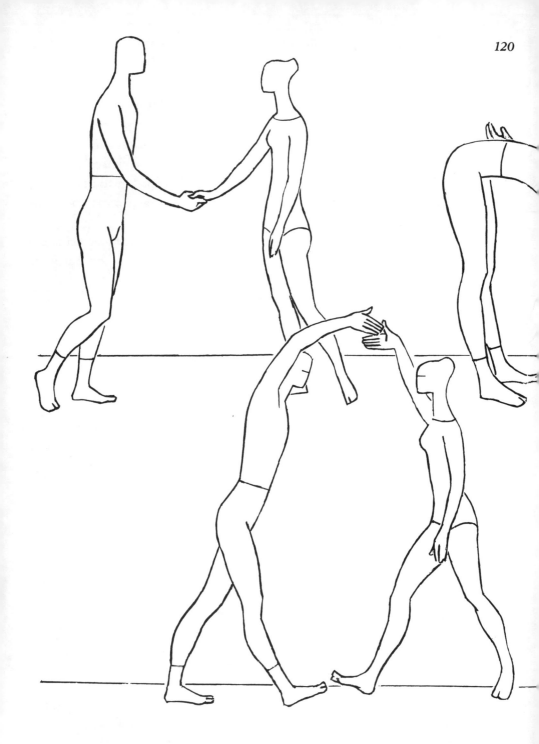

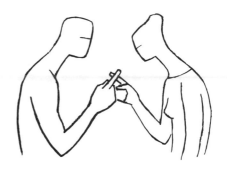

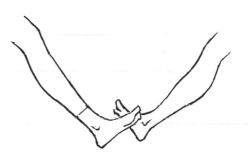

Stylization
of Handshake

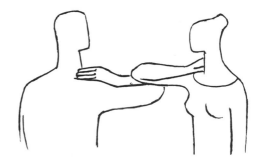

If any one element is changed, the whole import of the handshake alters with it to a startling degree. Suppose we just change the phrase. Put the climax at the beginning by emphasizing the thrust forward of the hands, through, say, a larger movement, beginning farther back with the arm, and with the participants standing farther apart. This gives it a fake look of inappropriate eagerness, or even comic gaucherie. For another phrase, put the whole thing on a monotone, so that there is no high point. This makes it wooden, unspontaneous. Then experiment with the motivation area. Remove the slight forward motion of the body. Immediately these two people are highly indifferent to each other, even hostile and discourteous. Bend the bodies back slightly and they look like insufferable stuffed shirts bursting with ego. Tilt one or both bodies to the side and a curious distortion results. This is so abnormal as to look eccentric. People do not say "How do you do" on a slant, unless they are trying desperately to be different, or are slightly touched in the head, or are in a high wind. And so on down the line. The changes in every element radically alter the meaning. This has to do with stylization because it removes the movement from the normal. But suppose we want to retain all the original meanings and merely make the handshake into movement for dance. A myriad choices for doing this will be at the finger tips of the choreographer. Experiment with the rhythm, just as an example. Prolong the handshake, in a much slower tempo, or repeat it several times in the original timing. Alter the half-quarter note timing; use repetition with a new rhythmic pattern, say eighth notes followed by syncopated quarters and triplets. The most obvious device here is repetition, which is the method most used for elongating mime into movement. The normal handshake lasts a second or two. By prolonging this through timing or repetition, we are immediately in the area of dance and not mime. Design yields a great many possibilities and can even be so elaborately developed that a whole section of a dance might be made in this area alone. A highly patterned advance could be devised, with the obvious intent of meeting. At the point of contact, innumerable changes in the design of the original could occur—for instance, touching hands very high or very low, more toward one person than the other, bodies facing front, side by side, bodies very far apart or very close together, and so forth. It is quite impossible to write them all down. One other important device, which I call substitution, is very useful. Instead of taking hands, use the same general contact pattern with the elbows, the feet, the shoulders, the knees or one finger, plus combinations of these things. The eye will still accept them as variations of the handshake.

Here, in microcosm, we have the whole process of turning mime, or natural gesture, into movement. There are two essentials, prolongation and distortion. This latter word is perhaps not the best choice, although the most accurate; as unfortunately, distortion suggests the ugly, the grotesque. Our treatment of gesture as stated above could very well be extremely funny, even bubbling with good humor.

Nevertheless, distortion it is.

This process, I believe, can be used for any gesture or emotional state whatever and will, in my opinion, be a sounder basis for dramatic dance than the emoting school, which feels vaguely and intuitively. Often the end result of this "digging" technique is quite different from that anticipated. For instance, putting the handshake through its various mutations may make it wind up being very funny where a serious idea is intended, or the passage planned to be tragic turns out to be pathetic or pompous. These are the hazards of composing, and are valuable in the learning process. The mistakes can even be husbanded and put away for future use, when the undesired result will fit into the scheme of a different dance.

In general, motivations in life and in the dance are two very different things. Every student and every dancer has been brought up morally and socially to conform to a religious or ethical ideal; good behavior is presented to him as honesty, compassion, friendliness, courage, sympathy, forbearance, cheerfulness, and so on through a long list of virtues. But the dance, as I see it, may call for the full gamut of experience, according to the theme. This means that the dancer must know about hate, revenge, contempt, despair, jealousy, remorse and all the scale of unlovely passions men are heir to. So the aims of art and life are very different, and it is often difficult for the student to let himself go and cross over from the lifetime restraints of socio-religious habits to those of unregenerate man that are often demanded by dramatic ideas. He may be able to feel these things; but having always restrained himself from expressing them, he does not know the vocabulary for them. Nevertheless, he is drawn to themes of violence, they seem to be easier to bite into than those of sweet reasonableness. So the dilemma for the young dancer is serious. His idea of a Machiavelli may be so pale as to be ludicrous; he has no conception of evil. Much time must be spent in the exploration of the darker areas, which calls for a divorce from what his mother and his teachers told him about being "nice."

Assignment

Bring an emotional study based on unpatterned movement.

Bring four gesture studies based on the four categories of specific patterns. Be prepared to show the original natural-movement source.

Words

14 Dance is the only one of the theater arts which has been divorced from words, whereas opera, musical comedy, drama and choral music live and thrive entirely or extensively because of their wedding to words. This, I think, leaves dance much the poorer, just as it would be unfortunate for a human being to be bereft of speech. This separation occurred very early, so that, shortly after the Greek era, dancing in the theater became an adjunct to the masque, the play, the opera. By the seventeenth century, ballets were spectacles of movement only. Indeed, the dance in many theatrical quarters was very unimportant, merely a divertissement in an opera, or part of a "variety night's" entertainment. Moreover, dance became the special target of religious bans and sank even lower, discredited and branded as immoral. Puritans in England and later in America fulminated against such innocent diversions as a Maypole dance, and to this day the actor and the dancer are still not quite acceptable socially because of their lingering and unwarranted reputation as loose-living rascals. Ask any average parents how they would feel about their son's becoming a professional dancer, and the horror you see in their faces goes straight back to the day when "immoral" was synonymous with "dance."

But to return to words. I see no reason against, and many for, an amalgamation of the spoken, sung or chanted word with movement. The purists who profess to be outraged by such an idea seem to me not so much prejudiced as outmoded. Why should dancers be condemned to be dumb? To keep them so is merely upholding the tradition, and maintaining what I consider an artificial "purity." True, the language of the dance is movement, but then the language of music is pure sound; and yet this does not inhibit the composers from producing cantatas, oratorios, operas and songs by the thousands, and endless musical numbers in shows. In short, combining the arts is such a natural procedure in the theater, that dance seems positively prissy in her abhorrence of it. Moreover, because of the rarity of the dance-plus-words form, the field has been very little explored as yet, and offers a magnificent country for pioneering souls. It was the modern dancers who re-introduced the word, and it is mostly the moderns who continue to produce an occasional work which pushes back the frontier. One must note that some ballet and show choreographers have latched on to this idea, after seeing the palpably successful and moving efforts of moderns from their early experiments in the twenties to now.

Several ways of using words have already been rediscovered. There is the narrator, who fulfills the function of storyteller and clue provider; the chanted or sung word by accompanying singers, or even by the dancers themselves, using actual dialogue while dance movement is going on; wordplay (fun with words); the word used as a climax to a passage, or as an inciting point, or just as a reinforcement of the dramatic line. There are probably other uses for words, not yet conceived of—a fascinating world indeed!

In the brief experiments I have made in this form, some fundamental facts stand out very clearly, do's and dont's which will save the newly converted from falling into grievous error. Chief of these, I think, is intelligibility. The sound falling on the ear must be carefully protected from obscurity, mufflement, strain. If a word is to be spoken or sung, the first requisite is that it be heard without effort. This seems so obvious, one would think that it could not be neglected; nevertheless, it is. Many a performance has a narrator off stage, using a microphone which the director has allowed to be swallowed alive by the music. Or, if dancers are speaking themselves, the high untrained voices often squeak to no avail beyond the fifth row. The director must constantly bear in mind that speech adds one more complication to an already complex theater piece using movement, color, costume, music, décor, drama, lighting; and the mixture can be very confusing indeed if the newcomer, the word, is thrown in carelessly like a second violin obbligato.

Then there must be the greatest taste and caution used in the selection of the words themselves, in respect to intelligibility. Choreographers have been tempted and seduced by exquisite poems full of the most fanciful images, and have innocently thrown these into the mixture in the belief that more imagination will make for greater magic. Nothing could be more disastrous. The poem we can read without distraction in a book, and re-read at will, thus tasting its sweets to the fullest. But the moment an audience tries to catch this over music in a one-shot chance, while movement is also going on, they are, at best, lost, if not downright furious. No, language must be very simple indeed. Leave out obscure images, please, and use no fancy unusual wording unless there is a dead stop while this sinks in by itself.

Narrative

To take up procedures in regard to various uses of words, let us begin with narrative. It seems to me that the function of the word here is to supply the facts: place, time of day, era, identification of people and their purposes, and like matters. The dance must be the area where feeling about these things exists, and emotional evaluation should not be in the words. For the dance cannot speak of some of the realities at all, while words can and do. To protect the dance, action ideas should be left out of the words; action is where dance lives, breathes and exists. So narration should not tell how things are done, or how people feel, but where, who and what they are. An example from the "Lament for Ignacio Sanchez Mejias," a dance I did for José Limón, is found in a passage about the bullfighter.

"Up the stairs went Ignacio, with all his death upon his shoulder."

This tells where, who and vaguely how, but it is left to the dancer to make it explicit. Incidentally, without this factual setting, the section would not be nearly as comprehensible as it is; it would look tragic, but not so fateful. In short, the word, to be necessary, must add information which will explain the meaning more clearly. Also, narration should be brief, must not overpower the dance element, or dominate the others too much. Long passages from books or poems merely make audiences restless if they are unaccompanied by action; or if words and action are simultaneous, the nerves tire and sag from the effort it takes to concentrate on everything at once. If words are going to be the point, then they would be better in a book or a play.

Song and Chanting

The human voice is probably the most appealing of all musical sounds, and song is a most sympathetic accompaniment for dance. In such a case it is not quite so important that the word be understood, if the general mood is clear. For instance, songs can be in foreign languages, and no harm is done as long as the action does not have to be explained specifically. I am thinking of a dance by José Limón, Kodaly's "Missa Brevis," all in Latin, sung by a chorus to organ music. Very few people caught the words, but it did not matter, as the mood was quite clear in the melody and the harmony. Besides, most people were aware of the order of the mass as a strictly traditional form, and they needed no facts from the singers. Contrary to this, a narrative song, like a folk ballad, would be an entirely different problem. Here we must hear the words or all is lost. Also, some manipulation of the ballad is often advisable, so that, instead of singing it straight through, the verses are alternated with instrumental passages to give the dance a chance to expand and breathe and explain, and incidentally to rest the ear and the nerves. The folk song can be otherwise fragmented, especially if it is so familiar that we do not need to be reminded of all the words. The principle behind this whole procedure is to open up the song, to add dance in the spaces and so make a new thing, the song with dance. Of the many ways the singing voice can be used, I recall successful dances which used ballad or narrative singers on the apron, where the voice was a part of musical accompaniment in the pit, and where the singing was done by the dancers themselves. In the very early days, I arranged a round, sung and danced by the dancers at the same time, in a composition called "American Holiday." I saw that this had great possibilities, but neither I nor anyone else has touched this idea since, and there are many other ways of making use of singing and chanting voices.

Dialogue

This is an almost untouched field, and might be a storehouse of treasure. Again, I see no reason why, if the folk ballad can be used successfully, a sort of dialogue, a passage using straight exchanges of words, could not be used. In fact, I am sure it could. Two examples of this come to mind, one a passage in my "Theater Piece No. 2," in which there was a satire on drama—two people engaged in one of those pseudo-profound struggles of a love affair. The action which accompanied the dialogue was not exactly dancing, but was dance movement. The other one is a short, amusing little jazz piece by Danny Daniels, in which three young people exchange talk while they are dancing. Here there is much more room for exploration.

Wordplay

Words can be fun, and with movement gain an added sparkle which is not found when they are used separately. At any rate, there is a special delight in their combination. I cannot remember any of these combinations of wordplay and dance on a professional stage, except by one choreographer who developed in my classes, but there have been plenty of them as a result of class work. For instance, in a short study in three parts called "Life," each section was introduced with words spoken by one of the dancers, and then interpreted. They went: "Life Is a Call; Life Is a Flower; Life Is a Cauliflower." Another was a game with different interpretations of one phrase, which was "Now and Then." The word "now" was accompanied by appropriate action, and was said repeatedly with a hollow and fateful sound, imperatively, pleadingly, and answered by a very flippant, "Now and then." Soon the question arose, "And then?" Again the imperative "now" was proclaimed; finishing with a frightened little voice that said, "Now?" This sort of thing can be great fun, and it is only in the combination of words with movement that the full flavor emerges.

The Beginning and the End

Words can place the dance in "when" and "where" and "what" almost instantly, whereas to establish this by other means would be much slower and less economical. For instance, in the opening moments of the "Lament for Ignacio Sanchez Mejias," mentioned earlier, the voices say, among other things, "At five in the afternoon, when the bull ring was covered with iodine, Death laid its eggs in his wounds." This is a good example of coming directly to the locale and meaning of the scene, which otherwise would be a laborious and probably vague sequence of movement. You cannot say, "At five in the afternoon," without words anyway, so why not use them frankly, and get on with the drama, the idea? This sort of thing is commonplace in musical comedy, where the dialogue introduction to the dance sets the relationship and the mood, and then the dancers go into the emotional realization of it.

Endings, or climaxes, are equally effective and equally dependent on the word for specific meaning. An example of this is in my dance, "The Shakers," when, at the peak of a crescendo of movement, a voice seems to burst spontaneously from one dancer, as though the press of feeling could no longer be contained in the dance medium. The words say specific things about the ecstatic state. Another instance is in the ballet "Facsimile," when the one word "no" is spoken near the end, at the climax of a passage. Incidentally, this was considered very daring for the ballet and provoked a storm of controversy.

Words Like Sound

Voices can be used just for their sound value—murmurings, burblings, cries, clickings, dronings and so on, ad infinitum. These can be most effective as an accompaniment to a serious mood, or can be very amusing indeed. The American Mime Theater does a pinball machine full of mechanical noises made by the actor-dancers, which is a gem of comedy. In another kind of dance, wails of horror can outmatch anything a musician can think of in terms of spine-tingling fright. In a dance of long ago I used four words, not so much for their meaning as for their percussive and rhythmic quality. They were, "Look, Speak, Work, Act," and as spoken by the dancers to music, in a syncopated pattern, they added not only a fresh sound to the ear, but meaning, too. The action showed that the attitude to the four words was serious and determined, but without the four words the movement would have been vague, at best.

In using words there is reason for caution, and as much understanding as possible of the difference between the arts of language and of dance. I have already noted the specific and factual function of language, which is impossible to achieve purely by the dance. Another great area of divergence exists in the timing. Words can bring images to the mind at a very rapid rate indeed, especially in poetry, which is often very compact. The dancer, faced with these concepts and their overtones, is very soon defeated if he attempts to follow the fast timing. There are two remedies for this: Avoid this kind of language and look for something slower and simpler, or edit the poem. This could mean leaving out lines or even sections, as well as conjunctions and the "verbalizing" of grammatic construction, and settling for key words. I feel no compunction in this cutting and editing of a poem, as it is all done in order to serve the concept of the synthesis of the theater. All the other parts of the orchestration have to be disciplined and made to conform as well. No one element must dominate or serve to confuse the others. This is what real theater means to me.

Despite the above, there are some ideas which can be conveyed much faster in dance than in words. The dancer can present himself to the eye as a human being, and, without moving a muscle, say instantaneously, young, blond, good-looking, sense of humor, well developed, tall, personable, well proportioned, long neck, head well set, All-American Youth look. This same person in a book would emerge gradually and over many pages, partly because it is no longer the style to describe the main character in detail in the first few paragraphs and also because words simply could not do it that fast anyway. Even the adjectives I have set down take longer to read than the visual impression of these things. To go on with our hypothetical dancer, the moment he begins to move, other instantaneous evaluations come to mind, such as: good feet, natural co-ordination, poor projection, bad hands, lack of elegance; but honesty and sincerity; cloudy imagination, insecurity, and a dozen other like thoughts. This would take a writer pages of dialogue and situation to expound, because in the language of narrative it is not enough to say, "He is honest;" it has to be demonstrated in experience. This is just what dancing does so quickly. It can say "honesty" and prove it on the spot in a few seconds.

In setting assignments for this sort of thing, I ask for very simple combinations, usually single words or short phrases treated seriously or satirically. Also, I warn again that the word must have a function, must add to the meaning indispensable information, or it is quite unjustifiable.

Assignment

Bring a study combining spoken or sung words, or voice sounds, for one body or a small group.

Music

15 Not all music is suitable for dance, and the appropriate areas are, I think, narrowed to three in number: melodic, rhythmic and dramatic. This leaves out a sizable part of the literature of music; the intellectual composition, made to illustrate a theory; the kind musicians call "eye music," interesting to follow on a score, but usually, dry and technical to the ear; the bravura piece, made to show off the virtuosity of a performer and the resources of a single instrument; the impressionistic composition, such as a tone poem, in which timbre and tonal color are the *raison d'être;* the "big" piece, such as the more opulent symphonies, overwhelming in complexity and volume and so complete that it is both futile and impertinent to attempt to add anything; the well-known programmatic piece, unless the composer's thought is going to be followed exactly; the too-complex composition in general, which is so demanding of attention that it cannot make a good partner; and, of course, the cliché-ridden and the commonplace.

In general, my point of view about good and bad musical choices is based on the limitations and special attributes of the art of the dance. It is a wordless art of the physical body, always speaking in its own ways of human beings, no matter how abstracted. It is not an independent art; it is truly female, needing a sympathetic mate, but not a master, in music. With this simple premise in mind, choices are clearer, and there is still a vast storehouse of music to consider, even after all the exclusions are made. The melodic, rhythmic and dramatic aspects of music are those most closely allied to the human body and personality: melody, through its original source in the breath and the voice; metric rhythm, through the change of weight of the feet and the pulse; dramatic sound, through the enormous range of emotion, always accompanied by a physical reaction. In dramatic music I include all mood sounds, from the most fully expressed emotional composition to the sparsest, and from elaborate *musique concrète* to the merest suggestion of tension of the plink-plunk school. None of this is intended to be danced "to" but only "on."

The choice of music, in theory, is fairly simple, but in practice there are so many complications to consider in a given situation that it is a major problem, to be met with all possible knowledge, experience and advice. It would be futile to make categorical rules as to procedures. Obviously the problems of the director of Radio City Music Hall are vastly different from those of the college student; but by putting a magnifying glass to a few specific situations, some inferences may be drawn that should be general guides.

Even at the student level, choices in music are complex. Let's say our novice is in a college fairly far away from the big centers of dance culture, where he studies (more often, *she* studies) in the physical-education department. Probably three quarters of an hour a week is spent on choreography, possibly augmented by a dance club, which is expected to give a full-length concert once or twice a season. The harassed teacher, herself with an incomplete dance education, must try to guide this young hopeful through the mazes of composition in a very few hours, and almost the first decision to make in regard to a finished piece of work is the music. Nine times out of ten, neither of them knows enough about it. Where are they going to get help, assuming that they know they need it? From the music department? Very unlikely. Those teachers are overburdened with their own problems. There are all those classes, the Christmas carol service and the chorale concert; and the president wants a centennial music festival arranged—or whatever. Besides, there is a felt but unspoken disdain for the dance, an inferior art buried in the physical-education department under hockey and basketball. The dance department needs some modern music? Send over Gershwin's Preludes, that's the best we can do.

The next resource for music is the young lady who is earning her way through college by playing for the dance classes. She is studying very hard for a degree in music, ninety per cent of which consists of the classics. Debussy is about the limit of modernism of which her teachers approve, and she is solid in Brahms, Beethoven and Chopin. But our choreography student wants music for a dance about an American girl faced with one of the many dilemmas with which she is familiar. Incidentally, I quite approve of her choice. It springs spontaneously from her "now." The pianist does not know of any music for this, but she would love to compose it. If the student and her teacher settle for that, the results are usually too painful to describe. Actually, the best source for music is the LP catalogue. The record companies have a magnificent collection of the world's music on display. But remember, we are in a minor college in a remote place. The riches in the catalogue are not in the college collection for the most part, and the local shop has only popular music and a few classics. This is admittedly quite an extreme case, but by no means unique. The wonder is that anything is composed at all, and that often the music fits very well in spite of the handicaps. The answer to all this is as complex as the problem: more up-to-date musical education related to dance for everybody, including musicians; the raising of the prestige of the dance to a respectable position; the assigning of more time to dance in the college schedule, as befits a great art; higher salaries for teachers, so they can afford a better education, and also so that more talent will be attracted to the campus.

Moving now into a more advanced bracket, consider the situation of the somewhat established choreographer who has battled and solved the problem of making a living while hanging on to an artistic career. To identify this individual further, he is a solo performer or he has a small company in ballet or modern or ethnic dance in the concert field; that is, outside the commercial theater or the big dance companies. To narrow his musical needs to aesthetic terms alone is quite impossible, for by now they are inextricably tangled with the demands of the practical. For instance, shall he confine himself only to the live music which he can afford? This means piano music or whatever single instrument is appropriate, or possibly a few other instruments on special occasions. Immediately limits are set in the choices he has. Not for him the world of chamber orchestras and choral music. There is no use in his dreaming of harpsichord concerti, and often, in relinquishing the music, the idea has to be abandoned, too. The alternative to this is tape recording. Now the whole panorama of five hundred years of music lies before him, limited only by what commercial companies choose to record. To be sure, there are drawbacks here, too. Canned music is undeniably *déclassé*. Musicians will sniff and carp, and audiences, though not so ivory-towerish, certainly do react better to the immediacy of live music. In a basic decision like this, between what one would like and what one can have, I should say, "It depends." If the choreographer longs to compose the piece for which chamber music is the only answer, then he should have it—on tape, and maneuver for occasions when this could be live. On the other hand, if he is not too unhappy with piano music, and does not wince unduly over arrangements and reductions which are sometimes unavoidable, he can enjoy the advantages of live music. The most important consideration is the creative urge of the choreographer. He should be true to this, and make what compromises are necessary elsewhere.

After the preliminary choices are made as to subject matter and music, there are important technical procedures to be kept in mind as to the fitting together of the music and the movement. I shall assume that our choreographer is advanced enough not to have chosen incongruous music, and is ready to start the actual composing with the right musical materials. Musically there may be two kinds: A live composer may be engaged to write a score, or already-composed music may be selected. The problems for each are very different.

Considering the latter first, the known score never fits exactly, but only approximately, what the choreographer has in mind. Immediately he hears it in the over-all, he finds that it is too long, or the slow section is too slow and too long, or it has a dying-away ending which does not fit the dramatic idea very well. In short, any number of things may be wrong with it from his point of view. He should first find out, in consultation with a musician, whether any changes can be made in the score without violating the integrity of the composer or of musical taste. This might mean the elimination of some repeats, or the changing of some tempi, or even adding a few more bars. One composer in my experience was prevailed on to add several measures to the ending of a well-known piece of his, in the interests of a more satisfying choreographic finish—and a better musical one, too, in my opinion.

After all possible musical adjustments are made, there probably will still be areas that call for ingenuity and imagination in the fitting-together process. In coping with these, it is essential to keep the ear sensitive, but also to remember that the dance is an independent art, subject to laws of its own which can lead the choreographer to movements not really indicated in the score at all. It has been proved over and over that these apparent inconsistencies, if done skillfully, will not only be acceptable, but will hardly be noticed if the dance part of the collaboration moves along absorbingly. As a concrete example, I was faced with such a problem in composing "Day on Earth" to Aaron Copland's Piano Sonata for the José Limón company. The third movement of Mr. Copland's striking score has a very long and very slow opening section, rather lost and plaintive, with soft dynamics. For dramatic purposes this was too long and lacked tension, but I did not hesitate to introduce some fast movement totally against the rhythm and dynamics of the music. This kept the narrative alive and I never had any complaints about it, not even from the composer.

A second example of the use of the technique of movement against the music illustrates other areas besides the dramatic where such procedures are justifiable. In composing to Bach's "Passacaglia in C Minor," I came to a long passage which I conceived of as a processional that covered several phrases of the eight-bar theme, the traditional form of a *passacaglia*. In experimenting with the movement, the right phrase for the dancers turned out to require nine bars, and was obviously damaged when altered to conform to only eight. My choice was to adhere to the movement needs, Bach or no Bach, with most unshocking results. Of all the thousands of people who have seen this dance, including musical purists, not one has ever mentioned this discrepancy in phrasing. In fact, I have to point it out meticulously, in using it as an illustration in class work, before it is noticeable at all.

Entirely different ways of treating music from a dramatic point of view could be described endlessly. In these instances, there is no attempt to adhere to the formal structure of the music, and the movement is set above the sound on the basis of emotional timing, which is very close to acting. One example of this occurs in my dance "Ruins and Visions," to a score by Benjamin Britten. In a certain passage the musical phrasing rises gently by thirds and octaves, pianissimo, passionless and almost mystical. At least, this is how it sounded to me after having listened to it dozens of times. But the ballet is on a very dramatic idea; and at the moment of arriving at this passage, the central figure has just strangled his faithless mistress in a melodramatic play-within-a-play scene. Remorse and horror attack him at once; so, to the mystical, gentle music, he moves in spasmodic, disconnected phrases of anguish. Curiously enough, the total effect blends and produces no shock. In fact it is more effective than it would be if the music were violent and emotional. It is difficult to say just why this is. Because of the dramatic line, perhaps the sound is interpreted as compassion for the anguished man, or for the slain woman; that is, as a universal pity for hapless human beings caught in the net of their passions. Or perhaps it is like a prophecy of the man's thin loneliness, which is to come. I am sure of only one thing: that the passage is convincing and that observers are persuaded to a different interpretation of the music from the meaning it has intrinsically. Also, I do not think the integrity of the composer has been violated, which would be unpardonable.

One other instance of dramatic treatment comes from a solo created by Anna Sokolow, with music by Teo Macero. The idiom is modern jazz, noisy and explosive. To this, a handsome, catlike girl moves very sparsely indeed. In fact, there are long passages where she does not move at all, but reclines and stares like a big sensuous animal. She does nothing to interpret the music. Instead, it is allowed to speak for her, or about her world, according to what meaning is attached to it. This is one example from an enormous area of collaboration between music and movement, very little explored as yet.

Most of the foregoing illustrations have had to do with the problems arising from the choice and use of music to fit a preconceived idea. But one can begin with the music itself. The attitude of the choreographer is at once completely different. He puts out of his mind any concrete images or conceptions he may have, and listens intently and devotedly to what the composer has to say. Sometimes dramatic ideas arise from the listening, sometimes visions of movement emerge; in any case the choreographer should not try to think, but put himself in a suggestible frame of mind. Once this process is over, however, and a decision has been made to go ahead with the music, all the skill in craftsmanship must be brought to bear as in other types of collaboration. The dance must have something to say of its own, and a mere visualization of the music is not sufficient justification for bringing it to birth.

One of the technical decisions to be made about the use of music arises particularly in the field of modern compositions. A good many of these are written in extremely complex rhythmic structures. Time signatures change very frequently, sometimes from bar to bar; melodies begin and end in the middle of a measure; syncopations are rife; often two rhythms are going on at once, not to mention harmonic complications. With a great deal of concentration, and a score to consult, this could all be analyzed and memorized by the choreographer, but I do not think this is necessary or desirable for two reasons. Because the memorizing will have to be by count, a very intricate mathematical sequence will be foremost in the mind of the choreographer, rather than the intrinsic movement materials which are the proper concern of his craft. Second, if the dance is to be composed for a group, and the choreographer insists on their learning all the counts—there will be real trouble ahead.

Trying to move with conviction and at the same time count a complicated score is so difficult for dancers that a shambles is likely to result.

Either the movement will be done well, but very inaccurately as to rhythm; or, by a glassy-eyed concentration, the dancers may be able to stay with the music at the expense of the movement and the feeling. My recommended solution to this is to use a technique which I have found practical many times. Don't try to count it—listen to the fundamental pulse, the sound of the phrase endings and beginnings, the over-all "feel," and utilize a direct-cue device for keeping a group together. By following one dancer in a key position, a group can achieve a surprising amount of unity and accuracy. This is partly because the body can be taught to memorize through the muscles. Once a movement sequence is set, it will be remembered in exactly the same timing at each repetition by even a large group of people. This achieves the same effect and is often better than if the dancers had been put through the excruciating and days-long process of memorizing mathematics and movement.

This technique is not always suitable, however, in cases where it is desirable to observe metric rhythms meticulously, and where these are not too complicated. The choreographer must decide whether his dancers are capable of grasping the rhythmic organization by ear or by count, and drill them accordingly; or whether a muscle-memory and cue technique will be more successful. In general I am against the count; this factual element tends to distract the dancer from his business of moving and feeling; and ideally the ear should be acute enough to get along without the mathematical tie. All too often, in a dramatic scene which is not very convincing, an X ray of the dancers' brains would reveal a Univac-like interior; there is no dance, only an image of moving machinery.

While we are still considering the musical needs of a fairly advanced independent choreographer, there is another way of going about it. He can have the music composed. Again, the practical circumstances are going to call for difficult decisions. Naturally, he would like to have the best, but inquiry reveals that music by top-ranking composers *begins* at a thousand dollars. Only large, subsidized organizations can afford prices like this for music, and our choreographer knows it is out of the question for him. So he casts about for lesser names, of which there are a great profusion, and for the style, harmony and general tone among them which he is looking for. Also, he had better look for another thing: a sympathetic attitude. Musicians are the complex product of many schools of thought, at different stages of development, but the one thing they have in common is the conviction that music is the queen of the arts. For the most part, they are devoted to pure music, and a programmatic collaboration is considered *déclassé*. This means that a given composer, not being fundamentally interested in writing for dance, is likely to have on his mind the suite that can later be rearranged for orchestra alone rather than a wedding of dance and music.

Even if he is interested in writing such a score, since this would give him a hearing, he knows nothing about it. Our choreographer should judge not only the music, but also the man. In the very close relationship which this is to be, is he willing to learn, listen and collaborate? Can they discuss problems and arrive at mutual understanding?

Here I would like to make a slight digression to state a few opinions about the training of our young musicians. This will be mostly in the area which concerns me, that of composing for dance. As to the rest of their education, I do not presume to comment.

It seems to me that the attitude of most music schools is unrealistic and reactionary in regard to their young charges. The training is traditional in the concentration on pure music, although the administration knows very well that the possibility of the students' earning a living composing for the concert stage is extremely unlikely. (I will leave out the performing and teaching and conducting areas as being outside this discussion.) Of course there are never many students talented in composition, but what few there are, are guided in chamber and orchestral composition, and maybe a little choral music. They know next to nothing about writing opera, or movie music, or dance scores, or television, or musicals—or about any area where music is actually needed, bought and paid for. All these activities, which might earn the talented composer a living, are frowned on as inferior by his teachers, who are bound to uphold the tradition, and who know nothing about them, either. Students are so indoctrinated with this attitude that they scorn them, too. Only a few music schools have a dance department at all, and if they do, it is only tolerated as an *avant-garde* idea. I am sure it is unheard of for a young composer to be instructed to attend a class in choreography, or to learn about the theory and practice of movement, or to analyze the scores already composed for dance. In fact he is so insulated that he sees very little dance at all, even in performance, and only incidentally is he likely to know about such works as Tschaikovsky's "Waltz of the Flowers" (dance music is so inferior!). Young composers, on graduation, are turned loose with a classical education and the smug assumption that they have all the equipment necessary to compete in the big musical world. That they do survive and often prosper must be due to extreme intelligence, aggressiveness, flexibility and curiosity, none of which they could have learned in school. Every other art training takes cognizance of the real world the student will enter. Dance, painting, architecture, literature all have both fine and applied courses to offer. The music school, on the other hand, seems to me too cloistered, wrapped in medieval ideas of aristocratic intellectualism, unmixed with vulgar education for persons who engage in trade. The Juilliard School of Music must be noted as a halfhearted exception to this.

The dance student, on the other hand, is exposed to music from the beginning to the end of his training. Even if he never takes a formal course in music, he has been hearing, absorbing and working to it from the time he first stepped into a studio. Willy-nilly, he knows something about rhythm, phrase and harmony and their psychological implications, from listening to music day after day, and from those sharp admonitions of his teacher: "You're off the beat," "You're not with the phrase," "That's not smooth, like the music." Also he sees many dance performances—the only limitations being his pocketbook and his environment—all accompanied by music which forms his taste and opinions. Admittedly this is not enough, especially for a budding choreographer, who should have an extensive musical education, but at least he knows something about his future mate.

Let us go back to the problems that occur when a composer who knows nothing about dancing is engaged by a choreographer who knows at least something, and possibly much, about music. The latter should take pains to speak in the language of music. For instance, words like allegro and staccato are going to mean much more to the musician than, "Here I do a series of rélevés in second position," and andante doloroso is better than "sort of slow and sad." This takes an effort, because for the dancer to describe in words what he has in mind is quite alien to him. I have watched many students try to tell a pianist what kind of music they want improvised for a study. They are likely to say, "I come in and move to here, and then I do a fall and some turns, and then . . ." Their voices trail off into a vague gesture or two. This sort of thing would be funny if it were not so appallingly ignorant.

So I recommend to the student—and this applies to advanced choreographers, too—that he stand with his hands behind his back, and describe in words, musical terms if possible, first the over-all idea; then changes of mood, if any, with their approximate length; the tempi of various parts, along with crescendi, decrescendi, and ritardandi; the rhythm; and the ending. These elements could be expanded in description for a major work, but the essentials would be the same.

Further suggestions for collaboration at the advanced level: Give the composer some freedom; don't confront him with finished choreography, complete in rhythm and other detail, and say, "Make notes on all this and write an accompaniment." This will not only be very irritating, but will preclude any collaboration, which the composer-choreographer relationship should have. I believe the right way is to have a preliminary conference, many if necessary, in which the choreographer explains his idea and the general shape. Approximate length of scenes or sections, in minutes, should be agreed on, and within this framework the composer should be free to carry out his musical ideas. Also, the choreographer will probably need to explain his conception of the relationship of music to movement: whether he will expect or want a oneness between them, or will welcome contrast; also whether, for the given idea, he prefers melodic, rhythmic or dramatic structure, and his preferences in harmony. If, by any chance, this composer does know something about dancing, and has ideas of his own, so much the better.

Even after fundamentals have been agreed on, it is advisable to make a few preliminary tests as to the mutual understanding between composer and choreographer. This is because of the ambiguity of words. It may not have been possible to pin down exactly what tempi are suitable, when these details are left to differences of interpretation of slow, allegro or presto. This could be made precise with a metronome, but there is an inflexibility about a metronome which is objectionable. Besides, they may each have made a mistake in judgment. A common error of the choreographer is to imagine movement in a faster tempo than it can be done, and the musician, too, even after seeing a passage or having it described, often writes the music too fast. So it would be well to experiment with a few phrases of the projected work. Other misunderstandings due to words arise from the meanings each individual attaches to them—words like big, heroic, gay, mischievous, somber, are only approximate descriptions and differ widely in their interpretation according to personal experience and temperament. It is safer, again, to use the musical words, gracioso, cappricioso, funèbre, and so forth.

There is one other way in which music or, more accurately, sound effects can be used for dance—for dance can dispense with sound almost entirely and be done in silence. This approach was particularly popular in the twenties and thirties, when many were intent on proving the thesis that dance was an independent art and could stand alone. But these techniques still exist, and have a particular power and fascination of their own.

To begin with, the dance without music—the absence of sound on a program which is otherwise ear-filling in musical opulence—has a contrary effect to that which might be expected. It does not seem empty, or as though the bottom had dropped out, but increases concentration and attention to movement to an astonishing degree. I am thinking of one of my dances of this sort, called "Water Study," done in about 1930. This was composed for fourteen girls whose bodies rose and fell, rushed and leaped like various aspects of water, the only sound being the faint thudding of feet in running movements, reminiscent of surf. This was so striking that the Schuberts themselves—those canny showmen—put it intact into a revue called "Americana," where it was staged complete with blue cellophane floors, walls and front drop. We now come rapidly to 1958 and, passing over many other examples, to José Limón's dance, thirteen Mazurkas of Chopin, which opens with a section entirely in silence. So the original point, that dancing can stand alone, has been proved over and over, but the main virtue of the silent dance is its power to simplify concentration and rest the ear. After a section or a whole dance with no music, sound is new again and fresher than if it had been continuous.

There are dozens of examples of the uses of sound effects, which have been very effective accompaniment for the dance. *Musique concrète* is probably the most popular of these, but there are others well worth the consideration of the choreographer. These can be very special indeed, as, for instance, the opening part of "Inquest," a ballet I did about 1942. It was produced in a studio theater which had at the back of the stage a flight of wooden steps leading to the dressing rooms. To get the effect of people coming from a great distance in the streets of a city in the early morning, I had the group come up these steps and finally emerge on the stage. The only sounds were those of shoes on wood, which were arranged in rhythmic patterns, so as to come within the range of organized movement. I must say this was enormously effective, especially in a dim, dark light, but could hardly have been produced anywhere else. It is up to the choreographer to seize on special circumstances like this and mold them to his advantage.

Percussive sound with the hands is fairly common practice, too, and is very refreshing to the ear. I remember hand claps as a part of the score by Carlos Surinach for the overture to "Ritmo Jondo," and later throughout the first dance. The opening-night audience was more than intrigued; most of those in the first three rows kept standing up to see what that sound was, coming out of the pit. In another dance, "There Is a Time" by José Limón, there is a long section devoted to "a time to speak and a time to keep silent." It is composed in alternate parts of silent movement and a complex hand- and thigh-clapping dance to express "a time to speak." The latter is further enriched by a chorus of clappers and wood strikers off stage. Not only is this effective on its own, but the resumption of the musical score of legato strings on its completion is a welcome contrast. Sound effects will aid the efforts of an ingenious choreographer in many ways.

In general, there is no part of the dance which differs so much from time to time and from place to place as the choices and uses of the music which accompanies it. Isadora Duncan danced alone to whole symphonies. Now this would be unthinkable. In some quarters, romantic music is considered the only suitable style for dance; in others it is thought to be passé. Many dance directors think a strict adherence to musical phrasing and beat is correct practice and that anything else is unmusical. In short, there are vast differences in approach. The opinions expressed here, therefore, are not considered final—undoubtedly there will continue to be changes and discoveries—and they are only the views of one modern-dance choreographer in the eastern part of the United States in the middle of the twentieth century.

Assignment

Bring in a piece of music suitable to an idea for a dance, with an outline of the choreography.

Bring in an idea for a dance, and describe the kind of music that should be written for it.

or

Bring in an idea for a dance with sound effects.

Sets and Props

16 In the twenties I used to look at the magnificent three-dimensional sets of Gordon Craig and Adolph Appia, and think: This is the kind of theater for me. At that time dancing was largely done in front of painted back-drops (as in ballet) or against elaborate realism, as in "Chu Chin Chow" (the spectacle theater). Realism was used, too, in my alma mater, Denishawn, with actual American Indian houses and bazaar scenes. The abstract archi-tectural stage appealed to me, however; and by 1928, I was using a set of blocks of graded sizes on which to place my dances. These served as levels of various kinds, low, or piled high, and also as mountains, houses, doorways, windows, altars. In fact, they were the hallmark of the produc-tions of the Humphrey-Weidman company for fifteen years. Incidentally, they were so sturdily made that some of them are still in use for the repertory I revive from time to time. Not only does a unit set of this kind fit together mathematically in various arrangements, but its suggestive pos-sibilities are limitless. However, its main virtue—and this is true of any level that can be stood or sat on—is to raise the figure or figures, and alter the choreographic design in relationship to floor-level dancing. Immediately there is a set-apart look to the dancer on a level, even a small one, such as a chair. In the case of large groups, if there are big surfaces several feet high at the back, or wherever, movement can be seen above the dance on the floor—so that complex ranks of moving design become possible which would be out of the question on a flat surface. Moreover, dramatic values are strengthened immeasurably by the use of vertical space. After discovering the added joys and freedom of levels that came with the use of blocks, I rarely composed a dance without at least one of them. Architectural sets gradually became very popular in modern dance, and now a great variety of shapes arise to delight the eye and aid the chore-ographer. These have never seemed interesting or important to the ballet, possibly because of economic considerations.

As an example of the intimate connection between physical levels and choreography, I will describe an incident in my "Theater Piece." In this one, a comment on present-day behavior, there was, at one side of a horizontal string of blocks, a space in which an oblong box was set longways on two smaller ones, at the ends, so that an opening of several feet showed underneath it. The back of the oblong was open and faced away from the audience. In this there was a dancer whose body was concealed, but whose head moved just above the surface of the box, from one end of it to the other. Hidden behind the end boxes on the floor were two more dancers, who walked together, only their legs showing, across the opening from one end to the other. At the start of the scene, the head and the four legs moved together as though they belonged to one body, and after this had been established for some time, the head delayed and took off on its own, leaving the legs to their own devices. This was, of course, both surrealistic and funny, but my point is that nothing like it could have been done without boxes to work with.

One other example of the many uses of levels follows. This concerns the set for the "Story of Mankind," a dance I composed for José Limón. It was a capsule history of man from the primitive cave back to a cave in the atomic age. This called for many scenes, and a prop box which would suggest architecturally the several areas of the action. The box was ingeniously designed by Michael Czaja. In the Greek scene it was a couch; in the medieval scene it looked like a banquet table; in the brownstone age, with the addition of some small benches, it somehow seemed like a small parlor; and finally, in the end, Limón lifted the box, with his partner on it, to a vertical position and it became a penthouse with a terrace. Some of the action would not have been nearly so convincing or eye-filling without this versatile box. In fact, the choreography was designed from the beginning to make every use of the possibilities of it.

The technical difference between a prop and a set piece is often very tenuous indeed, but the niceties of name-calling need not concern us very much. The modern dance is full of the use of what we will call props: poles, handkerchiefs, skirts (manipulated), fences, mirror shapes (movable), swords, flags, scarves (from small to enormous), tables, chairs, books, umbrellas, and unidentifiable objects which are deliberately abstract or meant to be symbolic. These, to be justifiable, must never be simply decorative, but must serve a functional purpose which is highly useful to the choreographer. They heighten the action; lend extra meaning to it; even, in some cases, make the whole point of the dance. One example of this is in the part of Lord George Hell, which Charles Weidman created for "The Happy Hypocrite." Lord Hell is grieving in a park over the sorry state of his affairs, and indulges in a long lament with a handkerchief. This is both tender and witty, and makes delightful use of the possibilities of the prop. Moreover, it is highly stylized, using on the handkerchief all the devices one would employ in turning natural gesture into movement. I, myself, was enamored of props by 1913, when I composed a game of ball for some Greek maidens, and enthusiasm has never lagged since.

In trying to stimulate the imagination of students in this direction, I ask an assistant to improvise with a chair, or a handkerchief, or anything that might be around in a studio—say, a piece of chalk or a glass. Each of these simple things has unlimited possibilities for dramatic attitudes and movement. Surprising studies emerge from the objects that are accidentally at hand. In a music school where I teach, there was a set of bells on wheels. One of the students did a little composition about a slightly mad bell ringer who hit high, low and sideways with burbles of movement in between, and even went riding on the casters through the Elysian fields of sound. I hope the music school never finds out about this.

Props can be very important, and serious, too. Witness the highly symbolic sword-cross which Cortes carries in José Limón's dance "Malinche," about the conquest of Mexico. Or the rope which is fastened to the "figure of fate" in the "Lament for Ignacio Sanchez Mejias." This she uses like a whip, a sword, a barrier, a lasso, a symbol of power. Alwin Nikolais has whole dances built on the use of various props, some very serious, some for charm and others for comedy.

There is considerable opposition to these prop ideas from conservative quarters, stemming from the purist conception that dance should be nothing but movement, unencumbered by anything else. Adherence to this attitude keeps many a choreographer on an uncontaminated, conventional level. Contrary to this, one young product of my school of thought makes a specialty of dances constructed around both words and props, with, I think, delightful results.

The shape of sets, or objects used on the stage, is subject to overtones of universally accepted psychological meanings. The rectilinear block has all the same implications that the right-angle design has anywhere—sturdiness and power. In addition, it also has the stability of the symmetrical. But other shapes are used constantly and suggest other meanings. The long, thin design, whether made in curves, straight lines or what you will, has links with social evaluations. Tall, slender women have been the symbol of beauty and aristocracy for many ages in the western world. The rising spire of the church suggests spirituality. Long, slim lines in clothing are considered elegant and sophisticated. The silk hat on a man is more aristocratic than the cap. The design of many motor cars, in an effort to meet the craving for the long, slim ideal, has become so long and stream-lined as to be an exaggerated curiosity. As opposed to this, there are in-fluences at work for the small, the squat and the lumpy, so that the streets are also increasingly full of tiny, buglike cars. They are economical, but their omnipresence does not diminish the grandeur and elegance of a Rolls-Royce. Intrinsically, these shapes are not as beautiful to the eye as the long ones, but changing circumstances often make them desirable. Couturiers, desperate to make women buy clothes, will design short bulky gowns with the belt line up around the armpits or down at the knees, and they scream in their advertisements that those long form-fitting dresses you have are all wrong this year. These designs succeed temporarily, as women will fall for fashion decrees, but the ideal of slenderness remains. Millions of dollars are spent every year for weight-reducing schemes by unhappy people who have unbeautiful round shapes, all in the effort to meet the aesthetic standard of the slim look. All these associations between the practical squat and the idealistic long-slim have implications that work everywhere, all the time, particularly on the stage. Florenz Ziegfeld knew what he was doing when he picked tall, beautiful show girls to pin his fame and fortune on; the little soubrette can be cute, but real beauty lies in the long look. Props and sets, then, are no exception to this range of values and should be given careful consideration in respect to these niceties of associative shape.

There are dozens of other designs with clusters of values or meanings clinging to them like barnacles. The circle or globe has at least fifty dif-ferent symbolic meanings: endlessness, the ring, the crown, the ball (play-thing or the world), the moon, the wheel, the millstone, the rose window, the bowl, the cup, the plate, the teething ring, the nipple, the breast, the head, the eye and so forth. Crosses have an immediate association, first with Christianity and, behind that, with many primitive religions. Tri-angles and stars are symbolic: the Star of David; the mathematical sign; the romantic star of the poets; the fateful star of Bethlehem; the star-crossed lovers; and, by implication, stars of the stage and screen, the turf, society. "Stars" are everywhere. In fact, there is scarcely any shape that does not have some association, and nonrepresentational dancers and painters are forced to go to great pains to avoid these, which is no easy matter.

To get the "feel" of dancing with a prop or using a level, the student is asked to think of a very simple reason for composing with one of these. Elaborate ideas of plot or conception are to be avoided, and it is pointed out that wonders can be done with just a small stick, a flower or a chair.

Assignment

Bring a study using a hand prop, and another using a level, or combine the two.

Form

17 Having scrutinized in detail all the elements of a dance, thoroughly dis-
membering the body, as it were, the creator must then know how to put
the parts together again and make the dance a whole; even a knowledgeable awareness of the broken fragments will be useless if there is no
technique for sewing them together. Perhaps over-all form is the hardest
part of choreography to grasp; there are so many pitfalls. The mind must
be firmly disciplined to cut, shape and fit to a pattern, resisting discursive-
ness, the swellings of ego, the wavering emphasis, the tendency not to
think it through to the end. Not only must the attitude be as objective as
possible, but the choreographer must stand away from his work spatially
as well—first in a literal sense, of space between himself and the dance,
but also psychologically, so that he is sitting in an imaginary tenth row,
looking at his dance for the first time, listening to the music, and receiving
these impressions as an audience would, all just once through. Fantastic
mistakes occur from a failure to imagine the impact on audiences. On
several occasions I have seen performances in which a house was kept in
darkness, with no music and nothing but a yawning stage to look at,
through a three-minute costume change. This, of course, without any
other consideration, killed the dance deader than a mouse in a trap. Almost as bad is the brief dance in several parts, in which the curtain comes
down and the house lights go on at the end of every section. These full
stops halt the momentum, so the thing never gets off the ground, and has
to start from scratch each time and "rev up" the engines all over again.

Consequently, I say the first thing about form is continuity. Anything,
to be exciting, must build, and nothing should be allowed to damage this
—not costume changes, casting considerations, or lighting and set ideas,
no matter how brilliant. They are not worth it if everything stops cold for
them. I should say that fifteen seconds is the absolute maximum for
transitions, and even these should be filled with music, lighting, set
changes, or all three. Other composers in the time-arts do not make the
mistakes common to choreographers in this respect. The musician does

not keep us waiting; the playwright and the musical-comedy director are almost as concerned over "pacing" as they are over the piece itself. Why dance composers think they can dawdle is quite a mystery, except that they are mostly studio-born, and not really properly weaned to a stage. And the experience that three of the leading modern dancers had for developing this stage sense is no longer available to the younger composer. Martha Graham, Charles Weidman and myself were brought up at Denishawn, where each of us had quite a stint to do in vaudeville. Here everything was planned for pacing. The curtain went up for the act on the dot, and if you weren't there, it was too bad. There was no such thing as keeping an audience twenty minutes before beginning. There wasn't any "dead" time; every second was precious or the show would fall flat. This included the bows, which were artfully contrived to be fast and "milk" the audience at the same time. Before the last dancer was off the stage, the music for the next act was on. Do I see raised eyebrows and contempt for this? In my opinion the dance could be a lot less esoteric, and would be much the better for it if it took on some of the rough-and-tumble, tried-and-true aspects of the popular theater. Some of this experience is open to young dancers in shows and television, but concert dancers see little of it.

Continuity and pacing in a dance can be achieved in various forms. Although there seem to be some key shapes into which most dances fall, these by no means rule out new or different ones. They are rather like classic rules for composition in music, and I teach them as the indispensables from which to start. They are five in number, namely: ABA, which includes other musical forms, such as a rondo and a sonata; the narrative or the story dance, or the accumulative abstraction; the recurring theme, the keynote of which is a repeated idea, one aspect of this being the variation on a theme; the suite, several unrelated parts put together for contrast; and, finally, the "broken" form, deliberately illogical, in which lack of continuity in idea is the point. Most of the dance on view today falls into one of these five categories. There are some borderline cases in which, for instance, variations on a theme are combined with dramatic development.

ABA

A true ABA dance, or an elaboration of it as AB, CB, ACA, is very seldom seen outside the classroom. Some dances do begin and end in the same way, but they hardly qualify if they are A B C D E F G H A. These classic dance forms are obviously derived from music, which is a very sound guide, especially if this kind of music is being used. Good composers know how to build for continuity, contrast and stability. Early music was in the main derived from dance; and now, especially with the moderns, it has been restored to its original purpose, and they march together. The ABA is thoroughly formal, and is suited to the nondramatic dance. Drama, being a compressed bit of life, cannot very well begin and end with an A section, or all sense of development and change, the very essence of drama, is lost. Life does not repeat exactly; no two moments are alike, similar as they may seem.

Narrative

This is one of the two most frequently used forms, the other being the suite. It should follow much the same laws as drama with a situation or a premise, a development and a dénouement. Hundreds of "story" dances have been composed and delighted their audiences, beginning in the seventeenth century with the *ballet d'action.* They can and do range from the simplest fairy tale to the latest Freudian maneuver. They can even be quite abstract, as long as they have a progression. For instance, "Night" from dark to dawn can be narrative and dramatic as long as it is not made of disconnected images; "Flight" can range from desire, to fulfillment, to a conclusion—either blissful accomplishment or a harsh coming to earth. In short, the narrative form has a thread of continuity and purpose running through it. Dramatic dances can be for large groups, and run as much as an hour or more, or they can be solos of four minutes. "The Emperor Jones," based on Eugene O'Neill's play of that name, and composed and performed by José Limón, is an elaborate drama for eight men in a number of parts, and lasts some thirty minutes. It is about an American Negro who became Emperor on a remote Caribbean island and was killed by the natives for his arrogant ways. It has the classic dramatic structure of a premise, a development and a conclusion.

Of solos, probably the most famous of all time, although now largely unknown to the young generation, is "The Dying Swan." Here again is dramatic structure. We know from the title that the swan will die, but in the meantime we see the beautiful creature gliding and increasing in its soaring mood to the final flutters at the ending. It probably was not more than five minutes long, but in so short a time, it made Anna Pavlova the most famous ballerina in the world. Another, almost equally renowned solo was "Rhada" by Ruth St. Denis. Here a Hindu goddess comes to earth to sample the sweets of men, and returns, well content, to her niche as a deity. It also made the fame and fortune of its originator.

Dramatic dances, like drama, depend for their excitement on tension. There are various devices which are helpful in keeping tensions alive, so that the goal, the complete absorption of audiences in the unfolding, is achieved. One of these is the "planted" person or thing. Many a rising curtain reveals a set-piece or two, perhaps a throne, an altar or a doorway, which immediately suggests future action. Or a dancer will be placed immobile while other action goes on for some time. In the back of the mind, curiosity is aroused as to what part the motionless dancer will play. I am thinking of a ballet of mine, "Dawn in New York," in which the curtain reveals two figures lying in upstage niches, who enter the drama long after the opening sections have been performed by a group. This makes for greater tension than if these two had made an unexpected entrance. Expectancy and the unexpected are both attention-getters, and the skillful uses of each are unbeatable. In a dance of Charles Weidman's called "Flickers," there is a scene calling for flappers of the twenties, who move with what was considered sophistication in that day. Through them strides Weidman as a sheikh, whereupon they all fall in a dead faint. Here the unexpected was the right note. Had he been standing in sight all the time, the fun of his unexpected entrance into the scene would have been lost. In a later part we see his victim, now in a desert stronghold, helpless, guarded by two slaves, and we wait for the unexpected with interest; what will the sheikh do to her? And will the hero come to the rescue? This, of course, was hokum, based on the plot lines of early movies, but though the authors of those films were crude, they had plenty of know-how about tension, not to be scorned by modern-day sophisticates.

Props can be very intriguing, too. Place a hoop, a level or a doorway on stage and immediately interest will be aroused as to what use will be made of it. Who will come through the door, who will stand or dance on the level? Action is anticipated. It seems to me that these props should be functional, however; otherwise they are meaningless or distracting. I remember a dance in which the curtain revealed a very ingenious mobile overhead, which was turning and changing in that fascinating way they have. But the dance never had any relationship to it, no significance emerged from its inclusion; and after a while, when this became apparent, it became an annoying attention-destroyer, because it was merely a decorative idea.

All the devices of drama for development should be known to, and considered by, the choreographer. The delineation of character, the conflict, the flashback, the inevitability of the conclusion are just as important as they are in the playwright's mind. Nevertheless, dramatic ideas are the easiest of forms because there is a ready-made framework for them. Hence the myriad range of choices is reduced, and only those pertinent to the theme can be used. The major concern can then be the pacing and development of the idea. The "dance" dance is so much more difficult because everything—the sequence, the movement, the beginning and the ending, the form—must be invented.

Recurring Theme

This is a much less common idea for a dance. Theme and variations is the most formal aspect of it, but smacks of the classroom and is not much used unless the music is in this form. An outstanding example is José Limón's "There Is a Time," which states its thematic material in the opening section and builds all the rest of its many parts on variations of the same movements. Unfortunately, this escapes most people; what they see is a suite form, contrasted ideas of dramatic or lyric significance. This is because the eye is not sufficiently trained to remember movement themes, and will usually miss them completely. This form, however, is of great help to the choreographer because it provides him with limited choices. Too much freedom is bewildering and dismaying in composition as it is in other parts of life.

An example of a true recurring theme is a dance by Charles Weidman called "Traditions." Here the tradition itself is a stilted-movement passage which recurs in its original form a number of times, always saying, "I will cling to the tradition in spite of everything." Here there are no variations on the theme, although the tradition itself grows feebler as it is repeated. Folk ballads are musical examples of recurring themes, with their constant repetition of the chorus.

The Suite

This is really a musical form, but is so extensively used as a dance purveyor that it deserves a category of its own. Abstractions can all be lumped together and called suites, but these range from the clear and clean-cut to the opaque. They can be elaborate in the classic manner, like Balanchine's ballet to Bizet's "Symphony in C," or they can be the murky contraptions of some of the moderns. They cannot successfully escape the obligation for build and contrast, however. Any composition, to be satisfying, should have a beginning and an end, and abstractions in suite form will fail without these elements, as will any other dance. What has held good for thousands of musical suites, from the simple prelude and fugue to the symphony, holds equally true for dancing. The most common form is the moderate beginning, the slow center section, and the fast, exciting ending. Notable exceptions to this would include Aaron Copland's "Piano Sonata," which becomes slower and more tenuous as it reaches its conclusion, and the aforementioned "There Is a Time," which is known musically as the prize-winning "Meditations on Ecclesiastes," by Norman Dello Joio. I, myself, would think twice or thrice before undertaking a dance which called for a dying-away ending or no ending, and very little contrast.

Broken Form

Illogicality is often the very heart of humor; it is a delight for human beings to escape from inexorable reason and relax in the unexpected and the *non sequitur*. So broken form is a haven for comedy. The first example that comes to mind is Charles Weidman's "Opus 51," which had us all in stitches because of its zany unrelated ideas, and a solo of his called "Kinetic Pantomime," in which a game of checkers becomes a mess of sticky honey, and such like. This sort of thing can be quite abstract, too, by the illogical and unnatural use of the body. I am thinking of a dance by Sybil Shearer called "In a Vacuum." Here all the movement is disconnected from its natural sources. Small parts of the body, such as the hands and feet, move independently of the trunk and of each other. This gives movement a most grotesque look, because, actually, even a gesture with the hand in its natural condition is attached to or aligned in movement with some other part—the arm, the elbow or the shoulder. To isolate these movements and destroy their original affinities is to be truly in a vacuum of nonsense, and it is very funny, too. This could also be used for satire or madness—any irrational state—or for a clinical study of parts of the body.

It cannot be urged on students too strongly that an over-all plan is important. The framework gives a firm basis for choice, and prevents that original inspiration from petering out in vague meanderings. Actually it should bring more peace of mind, too; for even the intuitive dancers —those who do not like to think—are subject to blank stretches when the inspiration gives out and a gaping emptiness leaves them nonplussed. A plan would probably save them. Here, let me make it plain once more that I am not advocating the composition of "think pieces." Nothing could be drier or more redolent of failure than the thoroughly thought-out dance that shows the clinical effects of analysis at every point. Lest there be any confusion about this, let me state the idea more fully.

The dancer has a world of experience to draw from as subject matter: his own life and observation; the other arts, particularly literature and music; and numerous sources mentioned earlier. He should be a sensitive receiving apparatus, which at some point vibrates violently to one of these; this seizure amounts to his inspiration. In the case of some personalities, this wide-ranging sensitiveness is not even necessary. They can be quite enclosed in their own egotistic feelings, narrowed to personal affairs; and keep producing like a waterfall in this limited range by their very absorption in themselves. Theory is no substitute for enthusiasm and desire; the dancer should be suffused with a dream and a vision of that glorious thing, the dance, and invite his soul as much as any romantic poet. Naturally, there are exceptions to this. If he is engaged to do a job, then a clear-eyed look at the particular requirements is very much in order. It would do no good to go into a dream state over seventeen eight-year-olds in a summer camp, who must put on some kind of showing at the end of the season; or to try to put his current vision into a production of "The Pajama Game." In any case, it seems to me that a thorough knowledge of the craft, if it can be kept mostly in the subconscious, is invaluable in all circumstances.

By now, the student should attempt a major study, really a full-blown dance, and be encouraged to undertake this with a sizable number of people. Large groups can be handled on the same principle as small ones, except that more blocklike patterns can be used, and more simplification of individual movement is in order. One must be careful to watch the focus, as the eye of the viewer should be led to the important statement. Interference with the main theme is so well known in the theater that it has a name, "catching flies," so that the actress who maliciously wishes to destroy her rival's important speech has only to flick a handkerchief now and then to catch every eye and melt the concentration. This can very well happen in dancing, too. If the group, which has been reduced to almost nothing during a solo passage, makes just a few sharp hand movements, it can successfully nullify the main statement. An opposite composing procedure, a lack of intention in focus, in which equally important things are going on everywhere at once, can also be very upsetting and confusing to audiences. People grow very unhappy over this; they don't know where to look and are constantly aware that they are missing something on the right while they are looking to the left. This would be like directing all the actors to speak their lines loudly at once—rather amusing for a crowd scene, but not ideal for intelligibility.

In the department of catching flies, I remember having had to restrain Charles Weidman in one scene. He had just made an entrance as a small boy, and when I came in as his mother, he was down on his knees in a corner, catching a bug. This seemed like minor business, except that every eye was on him and not one on me! With some dancers, this could really have been unimportant, but with Weidman it was too funny to miss.

Assignment

Bring a group study in one of the five forms, to already-composed music, or without music.

(Assign definite forms to various members of the class, so that all five will be represented.)

Three

A SUMMING UP

Check List

18 Having had a chance in five decades to make many choreographic mistakes, and having observed other people make them, too, I have compiled a short list of checks for the composer, something like a pocket set of rules for true-ing up a work in progress. It is all too easy to become absorbed in one part of the complex act of composition, and, while the attention is fixed on that, allow fatal errors to creep in elsewhere. A final checking up on balances is a wise—indeed, an essential—procedure. These, then, are some reminders which have been learned by painful experience and which should help the choreographer to avoid some of the commonest mistakes:

Symmetry is lifeless
Two-dimensional design is lifeless
The eye is faster than the ear
Movement looks slower and weaker on the stage
All dances are too long
A good ending is forty per cent of the dance
Monotony is fatal; look for contrasts
Don't be a slave to, or a mutilator of, the music
Listen to qualified advice; don't be arrogant
Don't intellectualize; motivate movement
Don't leave the ending to the end

There follows comment and explanation about each item on the list:

Symmetry is lifeless

In the chapters on design, it was pointed out that shape, per se, has significance and that symmetrical design always suggests stability, repose, a passionless state, the condition before will and desire have begun to operate, or after these have subsided. Therefore it is never exciting, and if it is misused—that is, in the service of emotional sequences—it will weaken the dance and result in tedium. Symmetry is good for calm states of being, ritual, or beginnings; or endings, when a resolution is in order. Dancers, without compositional training, almost invariably fall into symmetry, as children do when they improvise. The child begins to dance with his feet, the arms held out at the sides. This is in response to an instinctive reaction of the body toward balancing; the imperfectly co-ordinated child is safer with the arms out on either side of the straight trunk, to offset the changes of weight in the feet. Moving in space, the child usually runs with tiny steps (this is safer than jumping from one foot to the other), still with the arms extended outward. Turns are often done with both arms over the head; this is also a safety instinct—all the body weights are over the center of gravity, and the difficulty of the turn is minimized. All these movements are symmetrical in design. Children have to be taught to skip with arms in opposition to the feet, where the weights, though balanced, are more precarious. Every teacher knows the child who can only skip on one foot. My guess is that his instinct is operating to bring him to earth safely, after that one adventurous hop.

Beginners in choreography behave exactly like children in their choice of movement, and unfortunately some of them never learn otherwise, but go on into elaborate group compositions in which each dancer uses the arms symmetrically according to the safe-balance instinct, regardless of the subject matter and the cluttered look of all-out arms.

The symmetrical design in form is by no means rare either—two to one side, two to the other. Overuse of symmetry is not only naïve and unimaginative, but also very dull. No painter would think of using unrelieved symmetry; he knows this is for decorative art, such as wallpaper, fabrics, rugs. The dancer, on the other hand, because his instrument is his own body, is caught in physiological compulsions, and the snare of feeling good—that is, moving without fear of imbalance—is most powerful. In children this is charming, but in adults, deplorable.

Two-dimensional design is lifeless

The human body is three-dimensional. If composition is to speak of people, even abstractly, as in a pure-movement dance, the full dimensions must be used if the piece is to look warm and alive. Nothing dehumanizes movement so completely as the flat, linear design. This can be employed intermittently in a composition without too much damage, and sometimes very effectively, as it provides a welcome contrast. Nevertheless, the choreographer should always keep in mind its devitalizing tendency. Two-dimensional figures, as in Egyptian friezes and Greek vases, have been effectively stylized from the original models to make handsome decorative art. It is no longer human, but this is well within the province of the artist. Dance can also do this, to a limited extent, although the actual body can never be distorted and stylized as much as it can be with brush and chisel. Choreographers err most often in deciding when to use the flat design. In ritual, which has been traditionalized so that feeling is no longer dominant, and in other cold and impersonal subject matter, flat design is the very device to use; but too often, through habit or predilection, it is chosen to tell of warmth and feeling, and here it is a dismal failure.

The eye is faster than the ear

The eye is a far more educated instrument than the ear, which, along with the nose, has been retrogressing in sensitivity up the ladder of evolution. This is simply because the eye is a more valuable informer about our environment, is exercised more, and therefore is faster. That is, it grasps complex relationships more quickly, and also retains a more accurate memory of them. Not only is the eye faster, but, in a contest with the ear, will invariably take precedence. So movement must take the spotlight; it must not be repetitious or lazily lean on the music to carry it along.

Movement looks slower and weaker on the stage

One of the peaks of anxiety in choreography is that moment when the studio-born dance is transferred to the stage. Immediately space works magical and often appalling differences. Distance has weakened almost everything about the dance. Dynamics are not so strong, personalities are dimmer, timing looks slower; and so, with the essential vitality lessened, it now seems too long. In only one respect is it clearer—in its over-all design, because the eye can now see the whole in one glance without shifting from point to point, which is inevitable in the studio. Also, there is a seeming illogicality in the fact that detail is much more apparent at a distance. One would think that small movements and inaccuracies would be easier to see at close range. Not so, in practice. For instance, lack of precision in ensemble movements, overlooked in a studio, stands out on a stage embarrassingly. In fact, it screams for correction.

The obvious remedy for all this is to remember to compensate for the expected changes in the studio—what looks there a little too fast, too sharp, too big, too aggressive in general will probably be about right.

All dances are too long

In all my many years of looking at dances, I can remember only a scant handful that were too short. And this includes all kinds of dances: ballet, ethnic, modern and jazz. Almost all of them would have been improved by cutting and condensing. Everybody seems to recognize the overlong composition except the choreographer himself. In teaching young students, it has been proved over and over again that those who sit watching the efforts of one of the class need no prompting from me to judge accurately the length of what they are seeing. I am sure this is true of a lay audience in general; they know very well when a work is overextended, by means of that automatic timer of boredom they have in the nervous system. But the choreographer goes obliviously on and on, no doubt because he cannot be sufficiently objective. His self-fascination is working at a galloping pace. His own invention, child of his body and his brain, is truly wonderful to him, a proof to the ego that "I am," and no less dear than his very right hand. Anything so remarkable is surely worth repeating in all its movement, and drawing out to its full glorious length. Recurring shocks from those who feel it is a little too long never seem to deter him, except at the cost of much agony and resentment.

There is one other remedy besides cutting for the overlong dance, and that is more material, more intensity, more invention; in other words, a richer mixture might keep the whole thing alive in its original length.

A good ending is forty per cent of the dance

The ending is a highly important affair, which choreographers should worry about fully as much as playwrights with their third-act curtain. The theater is a place where the last impression is not only the strongest one, but tends to color the audience's opinion of the whole—which is perhaps not fair, but it is a fact. If the curtain—that abrupt effacing of the color, action, music—comes down on a weak, equivocal or illogical conclusion, the first reaction is one of disappointment, and there is an impression of total failure.

It takes an effort of goodwill to remember that, yes, the beginning was excellent, there was a high spot in the middle, the music was appropriate, etc.—still that fatal ending remains a psychological blight so strong as to mark the piece as unsuccessful. We are so constituted as individuals that we passionately long to be satisfied emotionally with our theatrical fare, and the supreme satisfaction is the final statement. When the last curtain comes down, we don't want to feel puzzled or at loose ends or cheated; we want to be refreshed and stimulated enough so that we, too, can break into the release of physical action—clap hands and rejoice. This does not mean that endings must necessarily be devised for theatrical dazzle, although this is a well-worn and reliable cliché. Rather, it means that they shall be true and, if possible, surprising. The inevitability of the ending must be apparent, and if to this is added an imaginative treatment, there is a double stimulation. Beware of originality without truth, however. This will not do.

Monotony is fatal; look for contrasts

The choreographer who can choose from a wide range of materials built right into his natural personality is rare. Most people live and die in narrow grooves. They meet all situations with fast nervous energy, or moderately and calmly; they plod or they fly, they are thinkers or doers, optimists or pessimists. The natural human being does not and cannot react in all these ways to his normal state. But to be successful, the choreographer, along with the playwright, the novelist and the composer, must enlarge his personal range, must seek to use and understand attitudes and timings quite foreign to his natural inclinations. Specifically, the dancer whose normal physical timing is moderate, and who is reluctant to leave the floor, will be badly handicapped as a composer if he stays in this range, not only because it will lead to monotony, but because moderation is the dullest area of all. Very fast or very slow tempi are much more exciting, because they are further away from the workaday pace. For the mover-in-moderation to lift himself out of his normal rhythm takes a very great effort indeed, plus enlightenment and conviction. I am afraid this happens all too rarely, and so there are too many dances of the deadly middle—medium pace, medium dynamics, medium everything, and extreme only in their dullness. Moderation in all things may be a good recipe for living, but in dancing it is fatal.

Don't be a slave to, or a mutilator of, the music

Procedures in regard to music alter radically almost from one decade to another. Not only do individuals change their minds about the selection and uses of music, but opposing ideas are now held, now abandoned in various centers of dance throughout the world. Perhaps the only thing everyone agrees on is that there should be music with dance. At this point, my own opinion is that the choreographer should not follow the music bar for bar, phrase for phrase, note for note. The dance should be related to, but not identical with, the music, because this is redundant—why say in dance exactly what the composer has already stated in music?—and because the dance is an entirely different art, subject to physical and psychological laws of its own. The ideal relationship is like a happy marriage in which two individuals go hand in hand, but are not identical twins. On the other hand, the choreographer should be a great respecter of music. Arbitrary cutting and juggling of parts to suit his own convenience should not be tolerated. For instance, snipping out the second movement of a well-known string quartet for a solo dance is a stupid affront to a great art. So is that other blunder that recurs so often, stopping short at an arbitrary point where there is no cadence, or ending with the remark, "That's all I need." These painful errors, and others like them, call for heavy doses of knowledge, taste and respect.

Listen to qualified advice; don't be arrogant

Independence and conviction are glorious qualities, and where would the human race be without them? Americans, especially, have the Declaration of Independence built right into their history and characters, and I have no doubt that our great contribution to the dance has resulted primarily from this outstanding trait. But this is also known by our derogators as brashness, arrogance and crudity. One must admit that there is something just about this criticism, and that such traits exist in the dance no less than elsewhere. It is impossible to mark exactly where independence changes into arrogance; but, tentatively, shall we say it is at the point where the very young, who seem to their elders to be promising and only partly educated, declare themselves to be artists with no further need for advice? Or perhaps they do feel a little shaky and uncertain, but the ego prompts them to stand alone, even at the peril of their artistic lives. Considering that it takes an average of ten years to make a dancer, and fifteen to make a choreographer, a declaration of independence much earlier than this seems premature. I think it would not hurt these young people to listen a little longer, and to exercise some humility. But one can easily make a mistake in judgments of this sort. History is full of examples where youth defied the elders and their traditions, and lived to be justified. Still, in general, there is not enough listening and too much egotism, and this applies not only to the very young, but also to older choreographers who cannot admit, at their stage of experience, that there might be something they don't know. These latter composers have had to grow up with whatever talent they possessed innately, but now there is a body of theory which it would be worth their while to investigate.

Don't intellectualize; motivate movement

There is a great difference of opinion about this point in the dance world, at least in the United States. In fact there is such a schism that the subject calls for a chapter of its own. At this point, it must be obvious that I belong to the faction that believes in motivation, feeling and emotion, as opposed to the widespread notion that these things are not only unnecessary but outmoded. It seems to me that an intellectual approach, which is central and not peripheral, is out of place in an art which has, as its medium, movement of the human body. Intellectual concepts are for the world of fact, for mental exercises such as philosophy and science, and for the word arts capable of making evaluations, which are, for the most part, foreign to the dance. One of the examples of intellectualism is the imitation of other arts, notably painting, which, with its quite different values of static relationships, can put a blight of immovability on the dance. I venture to say that dance cannot be completely intellectualized without forfeiting its audiences and endangering its very existence. Fortunately, such a ruinous procedure is not likely to take over completely, considering the vitality of the human being. Communication in terms of nonintellectualized movement seems to me the desirable goal.

Don't leave the ending to the end

I have already stressed the importance of endings, and because of this I strongly advise the choreographer to consider and shape the end long before it is upon him. This will mitigate some of the disasters caused by vagueness of conception—lack of time, the ending that seems perfect in the mind, but that is not right in practice. The workmanlike procedure, with all its logic, is not the best way to compose a dance. Things are usually made in a series of steps: the assembling of materials, the cutting or shaping, the fastening together and finally the polish or paint. Choreographers should not begin at the beginning and plod through like this. The dance is not an artifact, but is shot through with intangibles of feeling, intuition, inspiration, and a special psychological attitude to the ending. There is usually a high resistance to thinking about the ending at all. This is somehow supposed to come of itself, probably because the body of the dance is mostly concerned with movement, where dancers are happiest, and is the part that gets long and loving attention. But an end, a statement, a resolution, is a conception which must be considered and decided on. This takes thinking, always a painful process and one that dancers avoid if possible. So choreographers go skimming along, the time grows short, the deadline is upon them, and no ending yet. Something is put together in a hurry: Do this, do that, anything to get it done and over with; after all, it's a beautiful dance, and the last minute or two is such a small part of it. I would like to persuade choreographers not to work this way. My recommendation is to stop in the middle somewhere and spend many concentrated hours, if necessary, on the conceiving of, the shaping and redoing of the final statement.

It would be well to state again at this point that I am not a believer in the starting and shaping of a dance with the conscious use of all the technical information which a theory of choreography implies. Hence the placing of this chapter as a check list, and the craft section, which precedes it, as a preliminary study. The dance itself should be long dreamed over, the instinctive movement invited, glimpses and visions welcomed to entrap the imagination. The strict technical considerations, one may hope, are operating subconsciously to save the choreographer from the worst mistakes; but on the surface all is rapt excitement, the discovery of a new country. With this procedure, the wail of the young, "Now I know so much about it I can't compose any more," will not be heard in the land so frequently.

Conclusion

19 Being not only a worker in the field, but an ardent observer of the scene around me as well, I have some impressions about the state of the dance, and some apprehensions, especially concerning the sharp cleavages in opinion about style and content. I am no lover of trend-spotting or prophecy, whose advocates can often be spectacularly wrong, but I wish to raise some points which can be considered questions, and which seem to be so serious as to call for careful thought by anyone who has the welfare of the dance at heart. Since choreographers are important people in the dance world, these thoughts are particularly directed to them.

Where are we?

It can be stated as a fact that the dance, in all its branches, has prospered and spread in the first sixty years of the twentieth century with unprecedented vitality. Not even in the early civilizations of Greece, Rome, Egypt, were there so many people involved; so much variety offered at all levels of recreation, entertainment and ritual (different, but still there); such prodigious systems of technique developed; such added depth and scope. It is a lucky accident and a proud thing to have been born into this great flowering. But before we congratulate ourselves unduly, let us consider where the emphasis lies in this spectacular recrudescence, and how this burgeoning compares to similar thrusts among the other arts. Is the art of the dance really doing so well?

Recreational dance far outstrips all other forms in terms of numbers of people participating in it. At any given moment there must be millions of people dancing, on shipboard, in hotels, ballrooms and in the studios of Arthur Murray and Fred Astaire. Ballroom teachers, of whom there are thousands, are by far the most prosperous of all teachers, numbering among their clienteles men, women and children by the hundreds of thousands all over the world. Next in popularity comes folk dancing, which also accounts for its thousands. Children are intitiated into its joys almost everywhere, and it is taught in places where other kinds of dance are frowned on as immoral or too sophisticated or unnecessary. Adults indulge, too, mostly corralled by folk-dance societies, which have sprung up especially in English-speaking countries, to preserve the old ways and delight moderns who are otherwise restricted in their physical life. For the bettering of people's lives and for the health of the dance, one can rejoice over this, but one must remember that it has little to do with the dance as an art. Those in an audience who have danced at the recreational level —and this includes most of them—can be expected to have a more alert kinesthetic response than those who have not. Also, choreographers can and do make use of folk, ballroom and tap material (another minor recreational dance form) for their ballets.

The next great bloc of activity in the dance field is in the ballet. From the time the Russians burst on the astonished world with their extraordinary art, there has been a gradual, if sporadic, building of interest at both the student and professional levels. Now schools abound all over the world, mostly in the western hemisphere, but also in such unlikely places as India, Japan and Indonesia; and dozens of ballet companies perform almost everywhere. In this great expansion, the twentieth century has one of its claims to supremacy in the art of the dance.

Following this, the world-wide movement in the last twenty-five years to save the ethnic dance accounts for thousands more participants. In all parts of the Occident and the Orient, especially in India, the neglected and often decadent state of the native dance has been a subject of concern to all kinds of people: artists, anthropologists, government officials and cultural societies. As a consequence, not only were these dances rescued, but thousands of young people were and still are taught the dance heritage of their countries. Moreover, these traditions have flowered in many professional companies, which bring their culture to far places. American Indians go to the Orient, Japanese dancers come to America, Chinese companies play in Europe. In most cases these very old dances are in the class of fine art, removed by centuries of refinement from their origins of folk or ritual inspiration.

And then comes modern dance. At the turn of the fabulous twentieth century, two American girls, widely separated in space and unknown to each other, had a vision of a new dance, with its roots in the past, but its expansive ideas firmly in the present. These two were Isadora Duncan and Ruth St. Denis. Their inheritors took the life-giving substance from their hands, molded it in ever-expanding ways, and made of it the contemporary art dance. This new form was born in the theater, was designed to be a communication on a spiritual level, and still bears only fleeting traces of other values, such as spectacle, entertainment, folk or ritual influences. The fact that this is the most minor among the arts of the dance has a major irony at its root. Isadora Duncan and Ruth St. Denis were repudiated by their native land, and soared to fame through the rapturous welcome of European countries. They streamed like meteors through the sky, completely eclipsing the ballet, and theatrical and opera dancing. The European art world in general fell into ecstasies at their feet, and only then did they come back and capture America. But beginning with World War II, their inheritors were disdained and all but obliterated in Europe. In Germany modern-dance geniuses had abounded, but the war forced many into exile. They were welcomed in America, which is now the stronghold of the modern dance. *Sic transit gloria mundi!*

All this is obviously a source of great satisfaction to dance lover , but the question is, on closer examination, how is the art of dance really faring? I submit that, on the whole, it is reactionary. The ballet, which carries the banner for the art, and the ethnic dance are admirable storehouses for the masterpieces of the past, a vast museum delightful to visit, conjuring up visions and versions of other eras, all in the pluperfect tense. To be sure, there are exceptions. Ballet choreographers are sometimes influenced by new ideas. Fokine put Isadora's skips and her soft arms in his dances; "modern" hands and percussive movements appear; even subject matter occasionally comes up to date. There are infusions of jazz, too, which give ballet a contemporary, if juvenile, flavor. But this hardly seems convincing to one observer; it's more like a montage put together with bits of this and that, amusing and ingenious, but without a point of view building from the ground up. I am aware of the counteropinion, that there are only two kinds of dance, good and bad; and that if various "good" bits are put together, the product is automatically superior. I am afraid this is hardly defensible in the light of the history of culture and authoritative opinion in matters of taste. Aestheticians and historians agree that the soul of a people arises from character—that mysterious substance which is the result of vigorous responses to native environment. The Greek civilization at its peak is universally admired, and thousands of books have been written extolling its ethos, particularly the magnificence of its art, the integrity of which is so apparent. Still, all the words cannot really explain why this culture arose as it did, and we can only recognize its integrity, and, it seems to me, emulate its values. The art of the Greeks was wholly sprung from the philosophy, the values and the taste of their time; Greek life was all of a piece.

Can we say the same? Are we really building a dance culture indigenous to the twentieth century? Some of it is magnificent, but are there not borrowings and combinings, which, though fresh and stimulating, are hardly sound? I am reminded of an original idea of a nineteenth-century artist, who exhibited a small replica of the Venus de Milo with a clock in her stomach. The statue was good, and the clock, too, but together they were a horrifying anachronism. The dance world is full of gimmicks like this, which could not possibly be more tasteless or less genuine.

The third form which has a right to be called art, the other two being ballet and ethnic, is known as modern or contemporary dance. The very least that can be said for it is that it was born in and of the twentieth century and seeks sincerely to represent our times, our attitudes and our dreams. I do not raise a question as to the value of the conception. Everything we know about past cultures points to the fact that great peoples invent their own arts, which change from age to age as circumstances dictate, but that they do not lean heavily on the past, nor are they given to much borrowing. The Romans, though eminent in other ways, have left us no art of merit, because they swallowed Greek aesthetics whole and regurgitated it cold and stiff. The modern dance is certainly contemporary and original. It has made an uncompromising break with the past, but it is beset with troubles and errors nonetheless. Some of these are internal, within the field itself; some have to do with audiences; and some with the detractors who are defenders of the opposition, namely the ballet and ethnic art.

Where Is the Modern Dance?

Beginning with attitudes in the field itself, there is a great schism in approaches to subject matter and treatment, one branch of which differs widely from the original basis on which the movement was founded. Is this cause for alarm, or is it progress? Put very concisely, the difference is between a conception of the dance as an expression of modern man, and the idea that it should be a complete abstraction. The founders, and the first generation of dancers who followed them, were firmly of the opinion that the proper study of mankind was man. (Isadora was concerned with her soul, which she found to be in her solar plexus.) But after that there arose a large faction which believed that the body was a moving thing in space, and that any overtones of meaning were purely coincidental. One can conjecture as to how this idea arose. For one thing, there was painting, a major influence; where abstraction, which was rampant, was met by loud acclaim from dealers and gallery owners. The development of painting is not our concern here, but obviously the up-to-date approach was the thing, and with painting being heralded far and wide as the voice of art, dancers by the dozen climbed on the band wagon. The fallacy here is an inescapable physical fact—the body can never look like an abstraction. Painters can make nonobjective shapes and lines, dancers cannot. They only succeed in looking like human beings abdicating their right to be people and pretending to be objects in space. Is it possible that this is a legitimate expression of the disillusionment of our time? Are people so bewildered and world-weary, so afraid of life and what it offers, that abstraction is a welcome retreat, behind which they need not think, feel or suffer? That, to me, is a very sad conclusion, but logical. A sick world will produce a sick art.

One whole faction regards the abstraction as a delightful game, to be put together entirely by chance. The only rule seems to be, "No collisions." As it can be different at each performance, it is no end amusing to the composers, like a game of chess, but without the logic of it. Also, this sort of dance is one result of the preoccupation with stream-of-consciousness art, which began after Freud, or possibly it is just plain laziness. What a blessed relief not to have to say anything or worry about form; just let it come! The greatest influence of all is probably the irresistible urge to be different, to resist the tradition and be "new" at any cost. This is at the raw prompting of the ego, which is adept at bolstering its desires with rationalizations.

Whether the abstract dance is a healthy progression is at least debatable, and calls for thought and discipline, not just feeling and partisanship, on the part of choreographers, who have the responsibility for shaping the dance in their hands. The original trunk of the tree is still there, continuing to put out branches and leaves, and fed by the original substance; but on it are strange, exotic blossoms and inorganic geometric shapes, growing at odd angles. The question is, do these really beautify the tree and delight the eye, or will future opinion reject them as not quite the thing? In other words, will the dance retreat further from life, or come to embrace it more?

In the long run, audiences answer all questions, not only in the modern dance, but in every kind. Even the most richly endowed privately or state-supported dance company cannot survive except by the acceptance of a public. This is part of the dancer's "now." The advanced piece of choreography which might be acceptable ten years hence, but which fails to draw an audience now, will never have another chance; it vanishes. Critics have some influence on public opinion, but the average theatergoer cannot be coerced into going to see something which does not reach him, no matter how the connoisseur may rave. Bludgeoning in the form of, "You must see this, it is great," can bring an initial rush at the box office, but if these guinea pigs are not excited about it, ensuing audiences will stay away with enthusiasm. Economic factors are a grim reality in the dance, and, indeed, in the theater at large. Ballet productions are expensive; directors must be cautious about *avant-garde* choreographers in order to survive. The great difference between dance and other theater forms is in the totally impermanent nature of the dance. The play is in a script, the opera in a score, and these can be dusted off and brought to light at a more felicitous time than that in which they were first presented. Dance notation may be a partial answer to this, but will not save the situation completely. The choreographer is chained to his own day. If he has a "draw," all is well, or as well as it can be in this extremely difficult profession. But if not, he must either choke down those experimental ideas or haunt the fringes of the dance world, where he has the privilege of starving for the applause of a small, elite clientele. The fact that modern choreographers in our country survive with their advanced ideas is due to their drive, their fanatical belief and a growing audience. I must refute categorically the opposition's charge that the modern dance is dying. This is simply not supported by the evidence, and grows as tiresome as the hoary prophecy about the Broadway stage, whose demise has been croaked about for decades. Nevertheless, modern dance has great difficulties to overcome in winning its way with larger audiences, and these seem to be of two kinds, one on either side of the curtain.

To go on about audiences, therefore: For hundreds of years they have been conditioned to think that dance is synonymous with pleasure. To trip the light fantastic is to be carefree and happy. Dance is for wooing, dance is for social fun, dance is to delight the eye and excite the senses. Poets have used dance symbolism over and over when they sought images for the description of pleasurable states. Shakespeare said:

> "When you do dance, I wish you a wave o' the sea
> That you might ever do nothing but that"

and at another time:

> "Hot and hasty, like a Scotch jig."

When opera threatened to become too serious and the plot bogged down in murder, revenge, hopeless passion or whatnot, the dancers were brought on to rescue the piece and add a little brightness to the proceedings. In four words, dance was for fun. Completely forgotten was the dim past, in which dance was at the heart of every aspect of living in a functional sense; and after the fall of Greek culture, not until the twentieth century has dance been anything but a light frill on the edges of western civilization. Against the face of this entrenched opinion, Isadora Duncan and Ruth St. Denis had the audacity to throw a well-aimed gauntlet. No wonder the world was astonished that these two considered dance, of all things, a serious art, made of soul-stuff. They danced about states of being —heroic, tragic and mystical—in terms which went far deeper than the current amusing charm. And not a male lover in sight! Heretofore he was the indispensable one who held up the ballerina and provided the *raison d'être* of the plot line. Actually, what made audiences flock and rave was not the seriousness of the art at all, but the profound beauty of these two. They happened to be physically beautiful, which has always been and always will be enough to assure fame and fortune. But added to this was a loveliness of spirit, what one might call a "mystique," which was so apparent as to be appealing to everybody. The novelties introduced by these dancers, the bare feet and limbs, the uncorseted figure, the exotic or classical costumes, only accounted for a surface sensationalism to the hoi polloi. But the keynote was a profound beauty, where before there had been only prettiness, and the western world rose to acclaim it. In one sense there was no break with the tradition in this new dance. The soul of it was still the romanticism of the nineteenth century, and so audiences, though stimulated, found themselves on the familiar paths which they had trod in the previous ages. There was no shocking realism and nothing to jolt them out of the accustomed enjoyment of grace and beauty.

And then came the first World War, which caused such violent reactions in all aspects of living. In the other arts this merely accelerated a process of change which was already well advanced. But the dance, always ten to fifty years behind in its ideas, suddenly awoke to the fact that there must be a new evaluation of the art. This awareness was mostly given to the inheritors of the original two leaders, and those who were peripherally influenced by them. The ensuing development of that part of dance called modern is familiar to those who know their history, but what we are considering at the moment is the effect of these radical ideas on audiences. The first impact might be likened to a head-on collision.

Suddenly dancers decided not to be pretty or graceful or romantic, and said, in their movements, "We belong to the twentieth century; we have something to reveal about it in the light of contemporary experience; the dance is an art with fully as much scope as literature and can tell about modern man as authors and poets do. We refuse to be confined to romance and beauty." That this was a shattering and repugnant experience to audiences proves to me that the dance had been existing in such an unrealistic never-never land for so long that people had lost the sense of true evaluation. They were accustomed to savoring the dance like a sweet at the end of a meal, but when it insisted on being pungent or salty or even sour, this was met by loud cries of disapproval. "We go elsewhere for this kind of diet," they said; "to literature, poetry, drama, painting. And there are always the daily paper and the magazines." And for the most part they turned a stony face to modern dance. This was also true of modern music and painting, but not so uncompromisingly or to such an extent, and for a very good reason. The other arts, in the nineteenth century, were predominantly romantic, in keeping with the times. Still there were rebels who refused to be stylish, and who were moved to create in other ways. An example from painting was Daumier, who was given to savage social comment and was not ostracized for it. There were authors like Dostoievsky and Gorky, who told the seamy side of the truth. Educated people were exposed to these deviations from romantic beauty, and recognized that the world was full of a number of things, which the artist had a prerogative to deal with. Thus the vast audience of art was somewhat prepared for new attitudes and a wider scope of subject matter, which emerged with a rush at the turn of the century. Nothing comparable to this happened in dance. The Sleeping Beauty slumbered on while the dance world admired her loveliness.

When she finally awoke and charged around her palace as a modern miss, in the twenties, actually expecting praise for such behavior, the shock to audiences was understandably immense. All appeals to logic in behalf of modern dance were not very successful. To say that dance should grow up, deal with contemporary life as the other arts did, was to be met with the age-old attitude that dancing was for fun; dancing should be lovely and graceful. To point out that the cultivated man would never tolerate for a moment reading anything comparable to the plot of "Giselle" in literature, or listening to half the music accompanying the classic dance in a concert hall, was to be answered with a shrug. This very curious anomaly still exists all over the world—the man of taste, who may even be a connoisseur in all the other arts, will abandon his values at a dance performance and declare that the *status quo* is perfect. And to a large extent, there the matter stands. Audiences are responsible for dictating the policies of dance companies; and the fact, in my opinion, that the art of the dance is highly reactionary in comparison to the other arts must be firmly pinned on them. Knowing many choreographers as I do, and being aware of their creative impulses as artists, I think they would be more daring and original if they could, but without audiences this is impossible. The specter of the box office is an inescapable menace and the power of good and evil is in the people. In the meantime, the greatest draw in the dance world among ballets is "Scheherazade," which, in the light of later developments and of what the dance might be, is no longer the mountain peak of artistic achievement the audiences think it is. To be blunt about it, this no longer looks exotic or glamorous or Arabian-Nightish; not even Nijinsky could save it now from looking like pure corneography.

And yet, in seeming contradiction to the above, the modern dance, the only form of the art which consistently tries to be contemporary, is prospering, against enormous odds. The big masses of people are not its admirers as yet, but within its less ambitious scope in production, and its more modest following, an economic imbalance, though often dipping toward a loss, has not been an impossible obstacle. By ingenuity and determination, modern-dance productions do go on, and more adherents are won every year. By this frankly partisan defense of the dance art of our time, I do not claim that it is without blemish or that all efforts result in masterpieces, which are neglected by a prejudiced public. Certainly much of it is mediocre and deserves no acclaim, but what art is without this bed of gravel, in which the gold lurks?

And so the final question is, can we complacently consider that the art of the dance is doing as well as it can? I repeat that I consider the ideals and techniques of the nineteenth century to have been preserved like wax flowers into the twentieth, and that the dance is perversely being made to look like grandmother's collection of china dolls, her camellias under glass and her other charming little keepsakes. The hectic efforts in some quarters to jazz it up and make it faster, bigger, brighter, just make grandmother and her toys look a little silly and pathetic. One is embarrassed to see her stripped to the skin and wearing false eyelashes.

I think all the branches of the proliferating tree should be examined with the heart, brains and conscience of the caretakers, and this includes the public, the choreographers, the business management, the dancers, students, teachers, government officials—in short, everybody who has even a passing interest in the art. And if these people—individually, collectively, or both—refuse to grow up, think in the present and make of the dance a living thing, our times are going to seem to history like a prolonged infancy, or a twiddling of nineteenth-century toes while the present turns to ashes.

Though the focus of this book is on choreography, which I hope will be helpful in that important part of the art, my own focus is centered on what direction the dance will take next, and what will be its fate in the rest of the twentieth century. Anything so vital as dance will survive, but I hope it will not lie long in this, its flushed unnatural coma, and that its inevitable reflowering will not be postponed so much in the future that not we, but only our children's children, will see it.

Choreography By DORIS HUMPHREY

1920	Soaring	SCHUMANN
	Hoop Dance (Scherzo Waltz)	INGENFRITZ
1926	At the Spring	LISZT
	Valse Caprice	CHAMINADE
1927	Sonata Tragica	CHAMINADE
	The White Peacock	GRIFFES
1928	Air for the G String	BACH
	Bagatelle	BEETHOVEN
	Gigue	BACH
	Pavane for a Sleeping Beauty	RAVEL
	The Fairy Garden	RAVEL
	Papillon	ROSENTHAL
	Waltz: La plus que lente	DEBUSSY
	The Banshee	COWELL
	Color Harmony	VAUGHAN
	Water Study	
	Saraband	RAMEAU-GODOWSKY
1929	Air (on a Ground Bass)	PURCELL
	Concerto in A Minor	GRIEG
	Life of the Bee (Droning Chorus)	
	Speed	
	Air Study	
	Jesu, Joy of Man's Desiring	BACH
	The Call	RUDHYAR
	Mazurka to Imaginary Music	
	Andante, Opus 13	SCHUMANN
	Etude No. 2	SCHUMANN
	Prelude No. 2	BACH
	From the Depths	MACDOWELL
	Andante Doloroso	BACH
	Tanz No. 7	SCHUBERT

1930	Breath of Fire	RUDHYAR
	Choreographic Waltz	RAVEL
	Descent	WEISS
	Gargoyle	WEISS
	Suite	SCRIABINE
	Drama of Motion	
	Salutation to the Depths	RUDHYAR
	Salutation	
	Bourrée	BACH
	Dances for Women	RUDHYAR
1931	Dance of the Chosen	TRADITiONAL
	The Shakers (Drum, accordion and voice)	
	Introduction and Allegro	RAVEL
	La Valse	RAVEL
	Tamborin and Burlesca	RAMEAU-BOSSI
	Three Mazurkas	TANSMAN
	Two Ecstatic Themes:	
	a. Circular Descent	MEDTNER
	b. Pointed Ascent	MALIPIERO
	Variations on a Theme by Handel	BRAHMS
	Eccosassaise	BEETHOVEN
1932	Dionysiacques	SCHMIDT
	Orestes	MILHAUD
1933	Suite in F	ROUSSEL
1934	Exhibition Piece	SLONIMSKY
	Pleasures of Counterpoint	ACHRON AND OTHERS
	Rude Poema	VILLA-LOBOS
1935	Credo	CHAVEZ
	Duo-Drama	HARRIS
	New Dance	RIEGGER
1936	Theater Piece	RIEGGER
	Parade	TCHEREPNINE
	With My Red Fires	RIEGGER
	To the Depths	RUDHYER
1937	To the Dance (or, Preludes to the Dance)	LEONARD AND LLOYD

1938	American Holiday	MAMORSKY
	Race of Life	FINE
	Passacaglia in C Minor	BACH
1939	Square Dances	NOWACK
1940	Decade, Part One	COPLAND AND OTHERS
1941	Decade, Part Two	COPLAND AND OTHERS
1942	Song of the West	HARRIS
	Four Choral Preludes	BACH
	Partita in G Minor	BACH
	Dance "INGS"	NOWACK
1943	El Salon Mexico	COPLAND
1944	Canonade	NORDOFF
	Inquest	LLOYD
1946	Lament for Ignacio Sanchez Mejias	LLOYD
	Story of Mankind	NOWACK
1947	Day on Earth	COPLAND
1948	Corybantic	BARTOK
1949	Invention	LLOYD
1951	Quartet No. 1 or Night Spell	RAINIER
1952	Fantasy and Fugue in C Major and Fugue in C Minor	MOZART
1953	Deep Rhythm or Ritmo Jondo	SURINACH
	Ruins and Visions	BRITTEN
1954	Philipe el Loco	SPANISH TRADITIONAL
1955	The Rock and the Spring	MARTIN
	Airs and Graces	LOCATELLI
1956	Theater Piece No. 2	LUENING
	Dawn in New York	JOHNSON
1957	Descent into the Dream	PETRASSI
	Dance Overture	CRESTON
1959	Brandenburg Concerto No. 4 (with Ruth Currier)	BACH

DANCES FOR THEATRICAL WORKS

1930	Lysistrata (with Charles Weidman)	
	Les Romanesques (Rostand)	
1932	Americana (musical revue): Water Study	
	The Shakers	
	Carmen	BIZET
	Aïda	VERDI
1933	Run, Little Chillun (Hall Johnson)	
	The School for Husbands (Molière)	
	(with Charles Weidman)	RICKETT
1934	The Christmas Oratorio	BACH
1944	Sing Out, Sweet Land (Walter Kerr)	SIEGMEISTER
1957	The Child and the Apparitions	RAVEL

List of Illustrations

Index